SCHOLASTIC

Now I Know My

WORD FAMILIES
& SIGHT WORDS

New York • Toronto • London • Auckland • Sydney **Teaching** *Resources*
Mexico City • New Delhi • Hong Kong • Buenos Aires

Edited by Immacula A. Rhodes
Cover design by Lindsey Dekker
Cover art by Mike Dammer
Interior design by Holly Grundon

ISBN: 978-0-545-77683-7
Written and illustrated by Lucia Kemp Henry

1 2 3 4 5 6 7 8 9 10   40   21 30 19 18 17 16 15 14

Contents

WORD FAMILIES
Short Vowels

Activity	Skill	Activity	Skill	Activity	Skill
1–2	-ag	17–18	-est	33–34	-og
3–4	-am	19–20	-et	35–36	-op
5–6	-an	21–22	-ick	37–38	-ot
7–8	-ap	23–24	-ig	39–40	-uck
9–10	-at	25–26	-in	41–42	-ug
11–12	-ed	27–28	-ing	43–44	-ump
13–14	-ell	29–30	-it	45–46	-unk
15–16	-en	31–32	-ock		

Long Vowels With Silent e

Activity	Skill
47–48	-ake
49–50	-ale
51–52	-ame
53–54	-ice
55–56	-ide
57–58	-ine
59–60	-ole
61–62	-one
63–64	-ose

Other Long Vowel Phonograms

Activity	Skill
65–66	-ail
67–68	-ain
69–70	-ay
71–72	-eat
73–74	-ee
75–76	-eel
77–78	-eet
79–80	-ight
81–82	-oat
83–84	-ow

Variant Vowels

Activity	Skill
85–86	-all
87–88	-aw
89–90	-ook
91–92	-ool
93–94	-oot

Diphthongs and r-Controlled Vowels

Activity	Skill
95–96	-oil
97–98	-own
99–100	-ar
101–102	-ore
103–104	-orn

SIGHT WORDS

Activity	Skill	Activity	Skill	Activity	Skill
1	all	23	found	45	little
2	am	24	from	46	look
3	and	25	funny	47	make
4	are	26	gave	48	many
5	as	27	get	49	my
6	ask	28	go	50	new
7	ate	29	goes	51	no
8	away	30	good	52	not
9	be	31	had	53	now
10	big	32	have	54	of
11	blue	33	he	55	off
12	but	34	help	56	on
13	by	35	her	57	our
14	came	36	here	58	out
15	come	37	him	59	over
16	did	38	his	60	play
17	do	39	how	61	please
18	does	40	into	62	pretty
19	down	41	is	63	put
20	eat	42	jump	64	read
21	find	43	just	65	red
22	for	44	like	66	ride

Activity	Skill	Activity	Skill
67	right	90	was
68	run	91	well
69	said	92	went
70	saw	93	were
71	say	94	what
72	see	95	when
73	she	96	where
74	so	97	who
75	some	98	will
76	soon	99	with
77	that	100	would
78	the	101	yellow
79	their	102	yes
80	them	103	you
81	then	104	your
82	there		
83	they		
84	this		
85	too		
86	under		
87	us		
88	very		
89	want		

Introduction

Welcome to *Now I Know My Word Families & Sight Words*! This big collection of activity pages will give your child plenty of opportunities to practice and master more than 50 different word families and 100 key sight words—building blocks that help lay the foundation for reading success. Best of all, your child will experience the joy of learning while developing the skills that will help him or her excel in school and become a lifelong learner.

Research shows that independent practice helps children gain mastery of essential skills. Each double-sided activity page targets specific skills and words for your child to practice. The consistent format will help your child work independently and with confidence. Other important features include:

❖ easy-to-follow directions to help build vocabulary and early reading comprehension skills

❖ tracing, drawing, and writing exercises to develop and strengthen your child's fine-motor skills

❖ appealing artwork that engages and motivates your child to learn

On the next page, you'll find suggestions for introducing the activity pages to your child along with tips for making the experience go smoothly. Pages 9–11 provide a close-up look at the various activity formats, and for your reference, page 15 details how the practice pages will help your child meet key early reading and language curriculum standards.

We hope you enjoy doing the activities in this book with your child. Your involvement will help make this a valuable educational experience and will support and enhance your child's learning!

For background information about word families and sight words and their importance in learning to read, see pages 10 and 11.

Getting Started

Each activity consists of a double-sided page that offers practice with a specific word family or sight word. Introduce the activity to your child by going over the directions and walking through its features. See pages 9–11 for more information.

Helpful Tips

❖ For ease of use, simply choose the word family or sight word you would like your child to work on (you'll find detailed information on the Contents pages), locate the corresponding page in the book, and gently tear out the page along the perforated edges.

❖ The only materials needed for the activities are crayons or colored pencils.

❖ Let your child complete each page at his or her own pace.

❖ Review the answers together and encourage your child to share the thinking behind his or her responses. (You can use the reference lists on pages 12 and 13 for checking your child's work.)

❖ Support your child's efforts and offer help when needed.

❖ Display your child's work and share his or her progress with family and friends!

Word Family Reference List

Use this list as a reference for identifying pictures that represent words belonging to the target word family (printed in bold) and for checking your child's responses to the "fill in the bubble" exercises.

Activity		Activity		Activity	
1–2	bag, flag, tag, wag; 1. sad 2. tap 3. flap	19–20	jet, net, vet, wet; 1. sat 2. got 3. pat	37–38	cot, hot, knot, pot; 1. hat 2. pet 3. goat
3–4	ham, jam, ram, yam; 1. ran 2. yawn 3. hum	21–22	brick, chick, kick, stick; 1. pig 2. chin 3. tock	39–40	buck, duck, stuck, truck; 1. pack 2. tick 3. back
5–6	can, fan, pan, van; 1. run 2. ham 3. men	23–24	dig, pig, twig, wig; 1. kick 2. get 3. wick	41–42	bug, mug, plug, rug; 1. dog 2. red 3. jog
7–8	cap, map, snap, trap; 1. mad 2. sad 3. cab	25–26	bin, chin, fin, pin; 1. fine 2. find 3. pine	43–44	dump, jump, pump, stump; 1. drum 2. down 3. job
9–10	bat, cat, hat, mat; 1. man 2. ten 3. sit	27–28	king, ring, swing, wing; 1. pink 2. stick 3. win	45–46	bunk, junk, skunk, trunk; 1. dark 2. honk 3. spark
11–12	bed, shed, sled, wed; 1. bad 2. weed 3. lad	29–30	hit, knit, pit, sit; 1. fin 2. kid 3. bite	47–48	cake, lake, rake, snake; 1. talk 2. snack 3. back
13–14	bell, shell, spell, well; 1. pull 2. spill 3. fall	31–32	block, clock, lock, sock; 1. soak 2. look 3. float	49–50	bale, sale, scale, whale; 1. pole 2. whole 3. tall
15–16	hen, men, pen, ten; 1. hand 2. tan 3. pin	33–34	dog, frog, jog, log; 1. lock 2. bag 3. pig	51–52	flame, frame, game, same; 1. come 2. time 3. fan
17–18	chest, nest, vest, west; 1. mast 2. bust 3. rent	35–36	hop, mop, stop, top; 1. pod 2. hot 3. map	53–54	dice, ice, mice, price; 1. slide 2. mine 3. right

Word Family Reference List continued

Activity		Activity		Activity	
55–56	bride, hide, ride, slide; 1. nine 2. dive 3. time	73–74	bee, tee, three, tree; 1. week 2. feed 3. need	91–92	pool, school, spool, stool; 1. foul 2. tall 3. doll
57–58	line, nine, spine, vine; 1. dime 2. pin 3. tie	75–76	eel, heel, peel, wheel; 1. fell 2. read 3. bell	93–94	boot, hoot, root, toot; 1. shot 2. hot 3. toad
59–60	hole, mole, pole, tadpole; 1. wall 2. stale 3. mile	77–78	beet, feet, meet, street; 1. sheep 2. bean 3. tree	95–96	boil, coil, oil, soil; 1. call 2. tail 3. all
61–62	bone, cone, phone, throne; 1. lawn 2. bun 3. come	79–80	knight, light, night, right; 1. rent 2. sting 3. mint	97–98	clown, crown, frown, town; 1. yawn 2. our 3. claw
63–64	close, hose, nose, rose; 1. note 2. pass 3. claws	81–82	boat, coat, float, goat; 1. flat 2. soap 3. got	99–100	bar, car, jar, star; 1. tan 2. care 3. tear
65–66	pail, sail, snail, tail; 1. maid 2. rain 3. pain	83–84	bow, crow, row, snow; 1. gown 2. now 3. throne	101–102	core, score, snore, sore; 1. bar 2. pole 3. phone
67–68	brain, chain, rain, train; 1. star 2. maid 3. raid	85–86	ball, fall, tall, wall; 1. smell 2. mail 3. tale	103–104	acorn, corn, horn, thorn; 1. barn 2. won 3. more
69–70	hay, jay, spray, tray; 1. pain 2. claw 3. trail	87–88	claw, paw, saw, straw; 1. jam 2. lawn 3. star		
71–72	heat, meat, seat, wheat; 1. team 2. heal 3. seam	89–90	book, cook, hook, look; 1. knock 2. talk 3. crack		

A Close-Up Look at the Activity Pages

You'll find several activity formats that repeat throughout the book, as described below:

WORD FAMILIES

✦ **Write the Word:** To practice writing, spelling, recognizing, and sounding out words that belong to the same word family, your child fills in the letters to complete each word. Encourage him or her to note the sound and spelling pattern of the words.

✦ **Identify the Word:** In this activity, your child identifies and colors items that belong to the target word family.

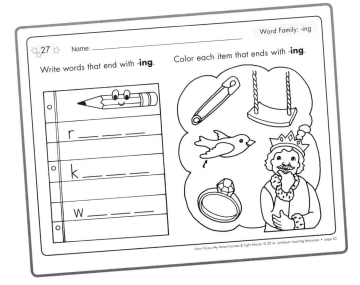

What Are Word Families?

Word families, also called phonograms, are rhyming chunks of words that have the same spelling pattern and make the same sound. This sound-spelling reliability increases your child's ability to read and spell many different words. For example, the words *top*, *mop*, *pop*, and *hop* share a common word ending, or phonogram, which means they belong to the -*op* word family. Once your child can read and write these words, it's much easier to learn the words *cop*, *chop*, *drop*, *stop*, and many more. By learning to recognize common sound-spelling patterns, your child can quickly and efficiently decode a large number of words and focus on the real goal of reading—comprehension.

✤ **Word and Picture Match:** By drawing lines to match each word to its picture, your child builds word recognition.

✤ **Bubble It In:** To practice letter-sound and discrimination skills, your child reads a series of words, then fills in the bubble for the word that does not belong. This activity also gives him or her practice with the format of many standardized tests.

✤ **Draw Your Favorite:** This activity invites your child to illustrate his or her favorite word from the target word family. He or she might draw a picture of something already represented on the activity page, or choose another related word.

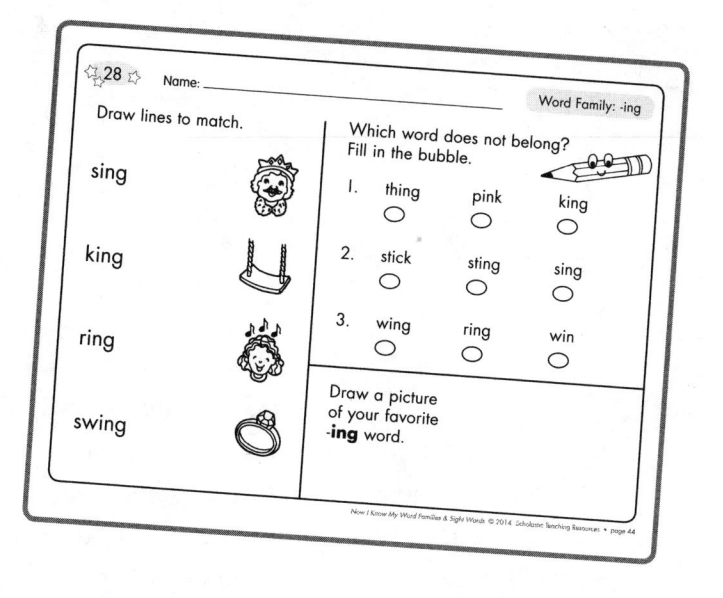

SIGHT WORDS

❖ **Trace and Write:** Your child traces and writes the target sight word. This exercise reinforces letter formation, builds fine-motor skills, and provides word recognition and spelling practice.

❖ **Color-Coded Picture:** This activity reinforces word recognition and visual discrimination skills. Your child colors each space that contains the target sight word and then colors the rest of the picture as desired. Some of these completed activities reveal hidden pictures.

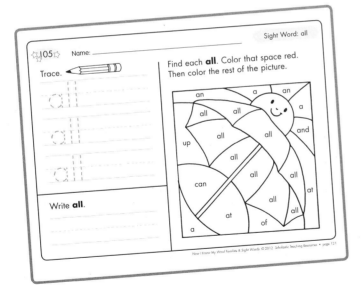

What Are Sight Words?

Sight words, or high-frequency words, such as *and*, *of*, and *the*, are the words we see again and again when we read. These words often do not follow regular rules of spelling so children cannot easily sound them out. And although many sight words generally carry little meaning of their own, they have a strong impact on the flow and coherence of the text we read. The ability to recognize these words "on sight" will enable your child to read more smoothly and at a faster rate, and ultimately remember more of what he or she has read and make sense of it. The words targeted in this book are found on the Dolch Basic Sight Word Vocabulary List, which accounts for more than 50 percent of the words primary-age children encounter most frequently in the print materials they read. For a complete list, see page 14.

Dolch Basic Sight Word Vocabulary List

Following are the 220 words that appear on the Dolch Basic Sight Word Vocabulary List. The words in bold are featured on the activity pages in this book.

a	brown	first	hold	me	**put**	ten	warm
about	**but**	five	hot	much	ran	thank	**was**
after	buy	fly	**how**	must	**read**	**that**	wash
again	**by**	fly	hurt	**my**	**red**	**the**	we
all	call	**for**	I	myself	**ride**	their	**well**
always	**came**	**found**	if	never	**right**	them	**went**
am	can	four	in	**new**	round	**then**	**were**
an	carry	**from**	**into**	**no**	**run**	**there**	**what**
and	clean	full	**is**	**not**	**said**	these	**when**
any	cold	**funny**	it	**now**	**saw**	**they**	**where**
are	**come**	**gave**	its	**of**	**say**	think	which
around	could	**get**	**jump**	**off**	**see**	**this**	white
as	cut	**give**	**just**	old	seven	those	**who**
ask	**did**	**go**	keep	**on**	shall	three	why
at	**do**	**goes**	kind	once	**she**	**to**	**will**
ate	**does**	going	know	one	show	today	wish
away	**good**	got	laugh	only	sing	together	**with**
be	done	green	let	open	sit	**too**	work
because	**down**	grow	**light**	or	six	try	**would**
been	draw	**had**	**like**	**our**	sleep	two	write
before	drink	has	**little**	**out**	small	**under**	**yellow**
best	**eat**	**have**	live	**over**	**so**	up	**yes**
better	eight	**he**	long	own	**some**	upon	**you**
big	every	**help**	**look**	pick	**soon**	**us**	**your**
black	**fall**	**her**	made	**play**	start	**use**	
blue	far	**here**	**make**	**please**	stop	**very**	
both	fast	**him**	**many**	**pretty**	take	walk	
bring	**find**	**his**	may	pull	tell	**want**	

Word Family Reference List

Use this list as a reference for identifying pictures that represent words belonging to the target word family and for checking your child's responses to the "fill in the bubble" exercises.

Activity		Activity		Activity	
1–2	bag, flag, tag, wag; 1. sad 2. tap 3. flap	19–20	jet, net, vet, wet; 1. sat 2. got 3. pat	37–38	cot, hot, knot, pot; 1. hat 2. pet 3. goat
3–4	ham, jam, ram, yam; 1. ran 2. yawn 3. hum	21–22	brick, chick, kick, stick; 1. pig 2. chin 3. tock	39–40	buck, duck, stuck, truck; 1. pack 2. tick 3. back
5–6	can, fan, pan, van; 1. run 2. ham 3. men	23–24	dig, pig, twig, wig; 1. kick 2. get 3. wick	41–42	bug, mug, plug, rug; 1. dog 2. red 3. jog
7–8	cap, map, snap, trap; 1. mad 2. sad 3. cab	25–26	bin, chin, fin, pin; 1. fine 2. find 3. pine	43–44	dump, jump, pump, stump; 1. drum 2. down 3. job
9–10	bat, cat, hat, mat; 1. man 2. ten 3. sit	27–28	king, ring, swing, wing; 1. pink 2. stick 3. win	45–46	bunk, junk, skunk, trunk; 1. dark 2. honk 3. spark
11–12	bed, shed, sled, wed; 1. bad 2. weed 3. lad	29–30	hit, knit, pit, sit; 1. fin 2. kid 3. bite	47–48	cake, lake, rake, snake; 1. talk 2. snack 3. back
13–14	bell, shell, spell, well; 1. pull 2. spill 3. fall	31–32	block, clock, lock, sock; 1. soak 2. look 3. float	49–50	bale, sale, scale, whale; 1. pole 2. whole 3. tall
15–16	hen, men, pen, ten; 1. hand 2. tan 3. pin	33–34	dog, frog, jog, log; 1. lock 2. bag 3. pig	51–52	flame, frame, game, same; 1. come 2. time 3. fan
17–18	chest, nest, vest, west; 1. mast 2. bust 3. rent	35–36	hop, mop, stop, top; 1. pod 2. hot 3. map	53–54	dice, ice, mice, price; 1. slide 2. mine 3. right

Word Family Reference List continued

Activity		Activity		Activity	
55–56	bride, hide, ride, slide; 1. nine 2. dive 3. time	73–74	bee, tee, three, tree; 1. week 2. feed 3. need	91–92	pool, school, spool, stool; 1. foul 2. tall 3. doll
57–58	line, nine, spine, vine; 1. dime 2. pin 3. tie	75–76	eel, heel, peel, wheel; 1. fell 2. read 3. bell	93–94	boot, hoot, root, toot; 1. shot 2. hot 3. toad
59–60	hole, mole, pole, tadpole; 1. wall 2. stale 3. mile	77–78	beet, feet, meet, street; 1. sheep 2. bean 3. tree	95–96	boil, coil, oil, soil; 1. call 2. tail 3. all
61–62	bone, cone, phone, throne; 1. lawn 2. bun 3. come	79–80	knight, light, night, right; 1. rent 2. sting 3. mint	97–98	clown, crown, frown, town; 1. yawn 2. our 3. claw
63–64	close, hose, nose, rose; 1. note 2. pass 3. claws	81–82	boat, coat, float, goat; 1. flat 2. soap 3. got	99–100	bar, car, jar, star; 1. tan 2. care 3. tear
65–66	pail, sail, snail, tail; 1. maid 2. rain 3. pain	83–84	bow, crow, row, snow; 1. gown 2. now 3. throne	101–102	core, score, snore, sore; 1. bar 2. pole 3. phone
67–68	brain, chain, rain, train; 1. star 2. maid 3. raid	85–86	ball, fall, tall, wall; 1. smell 2. mail 3. tale	103–104	acorn, corn, horn, thorn; 1. barn 2. won 3. more
69–70	hay, jay, spray, tray; 1. pain 2. claw 3. trail	87–88	claw, paw, saw, straw; 1. jam 2. lawn 3. star		
71–72	heat, meat, seat, wheat; 1. team 2. heal 3. seam	89–90	book, cook, hook, look; 1. knock 2. talk 3. crack		

Dolch Basic Sight Word Vocabulary List

Following are the 220 words that appear on the Dolch Basic Sight Word Vocabulary List.
The words in bold are featured on the activity pages in this book.

a	brown	first	hold	me	**put**	ten	warm
about	**but**	five	hot	much	ran	thank	**was**
after	buy	fly	**how**	must	**read**	**that**	wash
again	**by**	for	hurt	**my**	**red**	**the**	we
all	call	**found**	I	myself	**ride**	**their**	**well**
always	**came**	four	if	never	**right**	**them**	**went**
am	can	**from**	in	**new**	round	**then**	**were**
an	carry	full	**into**	**no**	**run**	**there**	**what**
and	clean	**funny**	**is**	**not**	**said**	these	**when**
any	cold	**gave**	it	**now**	**saw**	**they**	**where**
are	**come**	**get**	its	**of**	**say**	think	which
around	could	give	**jump**	**off**	**see**	**this**	white
as	cut	**go**	**just**	old	seven	those	**who**
ask	**did**	**goes**	keep	**on**	shall	three	why
at	**do**	going	kind	once	**she**	to	**will**
ate	**does**	**good**	know	one	show	today	wish
away	done	got	laugh	only	sing	together	**with**
be	don't	green	let	open	sit	**too**	work
because	**down**	grow	light	or	six	try	**would**
been	draw	**had**	**like**	**our**	sleep	two	write
before	drink	has	**little**	**out**	small	**under**	**yellow**
best	**eat**	**have**	live	**over**	**so**	up	**yes**
better	eight	**he**	long	own	**some**	upon	**you**
big	every	**help**	**look**	pick	**soon**	**us**	**your**
black	fall	**her**	made	**play**	start	use	
blue	far	**here**	**make**	**please**	stop	**very**	
both	fast	**him**	**many**	**pretty**	take	walk	
bring	**find**	**his**	may	pull	tell	**want**	

Connections to the Standards

The activities in this book support the College and Career Readiness (CCR) Standards. These broad standards, which serve as the basis of many state standards, were developed to establish grade-by-grade educational expectations with the goal of providing students nationwide with a quality education that prepares them for college and careers. The standards begin in kindergarten, so, if your child is of preschool age, the activities will help set the stage for your child's success with the following early reading and language standards for students in kindergarten, first, and second grade.

READING

Print Concepts

Demonstrate understanding of the organization and basic features of print.

- Follow words from left to right and top to bottom.
- Recognize that spoken words are represented in written language by specific sequences of letters.
- Understand that words are separated by spaces in print.
- Recognize and name all upper- and lowercase letters of the alphabet.
- Recognize the distinguishing features of a sentence (e.g., first word, capitalization, ending punctuation).

Phonological Awareness

Demonstrate understanding of spoken words, syllables, and sounds.

- Recognize and produce rhyming words.
- Count, pronounce, blend, and segment syllables in spoken words.
- Blend and segment onsets and rimes of single-syllable spoken words.
- Isolate and pronounce the initial, medial vowel, and final sounds in three-phoneme (consonant-vowel-consonant, or CVC) words.
- Add or substitute individual sounds in simple, one-syllable words to make new words.
- Distinguish long- from short-vowel sounds in spoken single-syllable words.

- Orally produce single-syllable words by blending sounds, including consonant blends.
- Isolate and pronounce initial, medial vowel, and final sounds in spoken single-syllable words.
- Segment spoken single-syllable words into their complete sequence of individual sounds.

Phonics and Word Recognition

Know and apply grade-level phonics and word analysis skills in decoding words.

- Demonstrate basic knowledge of letter-sound correspondences by producing the primary or most frequent sound for each consonant.
- Associate the long and short sounds with the common spellings for the five major vowels.
- Read common high-frequency words by sight (e.g., *the*, *of*, *to*, *you*, *she*, *my*, *is*, *are*, *do*, *does*).
- Distinguish between similarly spelled words by identifying the sounds of the letters that differ.
- Know the spelling-sound correspondences for common consonant digraphs (two letters that represent one sound).
- Decode regularly spelled one-syllable words.
- Know final *e* and common vowel teams for representing long-vowel sounds.
- Recognize and read grade-appropriate irregularly spelled words.
- Distinguish long and short vowels when reading regularly spelled one-syllable words.

Fluency

Read with sufficient accuracy and fluency to support comprehension.

- Read grade-level text with purpose and understanding.
- Use context to confirm or self-correct word recognition and understanding, rereading as necessary.

LANGUAGE

Conventions of Standard English

Demonstrate command of the conventions of standard English grammar and spelling when writing or speaking.

- Print upper- and lowercase letters.

Demonstrate command of the conventions of standard English capitalization, punctuation, and spelling when writing.

- Write a letter or letters for most consonant and short-vowel sounds.
- Spell simple words phonetically, drawing on knowledge of sound-letter relationships.

Write words that end with -**ag**.

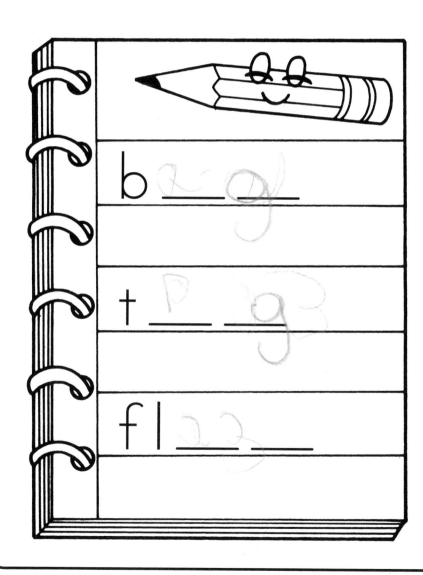

b __ __ g

t __ __ g

fl __ __ __

Color each item that ends with -**ag**.

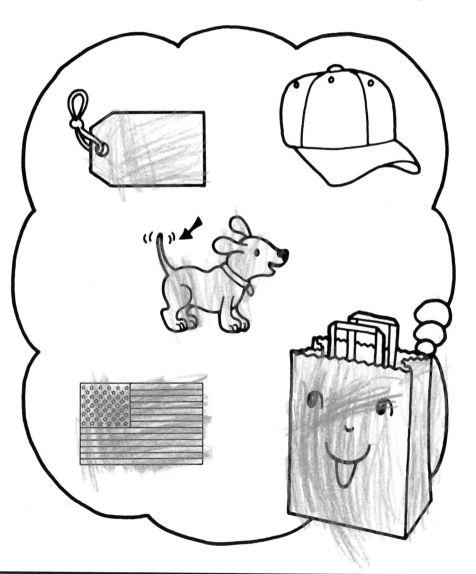

Draw lines to match.

wag

flag

tag

bag

Which word does not belong? Fill in the bubble.

1. sad   rag   bag
   ●   ○   ○

2. drag   tag   tap
   ○   ○   ●

3. wag   flap   flag
   ○   ●   ○

Draw a picture of your favorite **-ag** word.

Norad

Write words that end with -am.

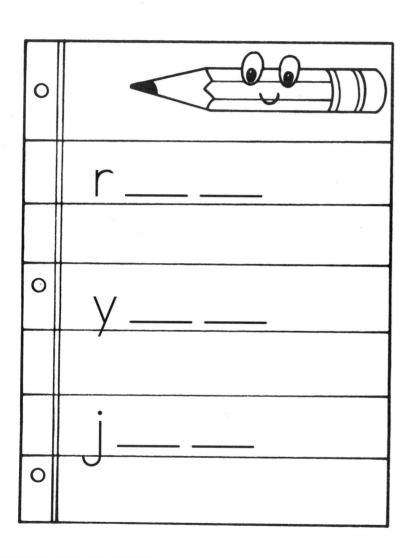

r _ _ _

y _ _ _

j _ _ _

Color each item that ends with -am.

4 Name: _____

Draw lines to match.

ram

yam

jam

ham

Which word does not belong?
Fill in the bubble.

1. slam   ran   ram
    ○   ○   ○

2. yawn   yam   clam
    ○   ○   ○

3. ham   jam   hum
    ○   ○   ○

Draw a picture
of your favorite
-am word.

Write words that end with -an.   Color each item that ends with -an.

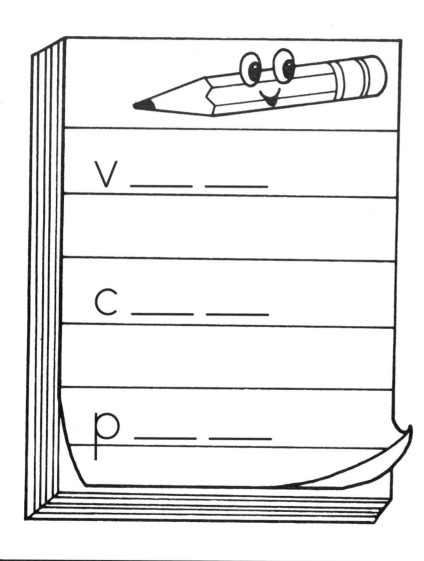

v _ _ _

c _ _ _

p _ _ _

Draw lines to match.

fan

pan

van

can

Which word does not belong?
Fill in the bubble.

1.   run   van   ran
     ◯   ◯   ◯

2.   man   tan   ham
     ◯   ◯   ◯

3.   can   men   fan
     ◯   ◯   ◯

Draw a picture
of your favorite
-an word.

AMY   Amy   Amelia

Name: _____

Write words that end with -**ap**.

Color each item that ends with -**ap**.

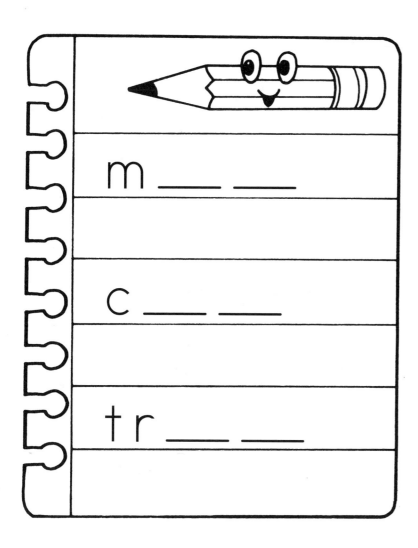

m _ _ _

c _ _ _

tr _ _ _

Draw lines to match.

map

cap

snap

trap

Which word does not belong?
Fill in the bubble.

1. map   mad   clap
   ◯   ◯   ◯

2. sad   lap   trap
   ◯   ◯   ◯

3. nap   slap   cab
   ◯   ◯   ◯

Draw a picture
of your favorite
-ap word.

Name: _____

Write words that end with -at.

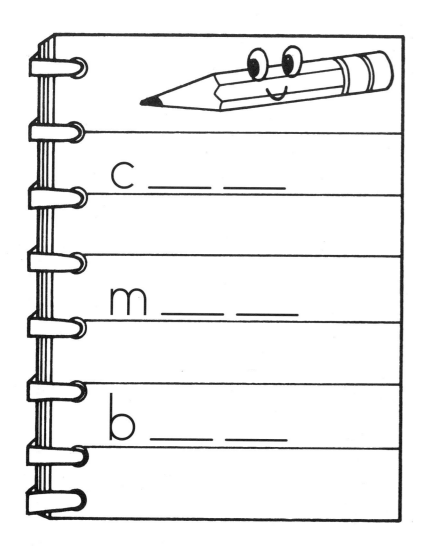

c _ _ _

m _ _ _

b _ _ _

Color each item that ends with -at.

Welcome

10

Name: _____

Draw lines to match.

mat

cat

bat

hat

Which word does not belong?
Fill in the bubble.

1.   mat   hat   man
      ◯   ◯   ◯

2.   that   fat   ten
      ◯   ◯   ◯

3.   sit   bat   sat
      ◯   ◯   ◯

Draw a picture
of your favorite
-at word.

Write words that end with -ed.

Color each item that ends with -ed.

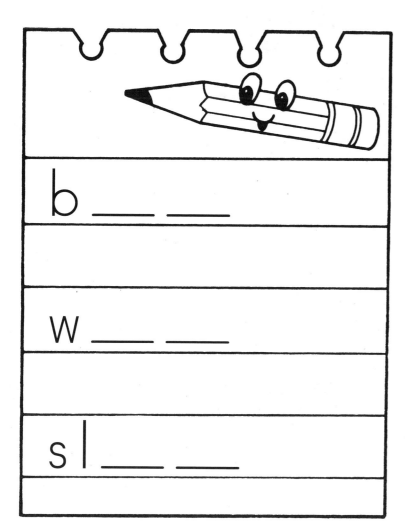

b _ _ _

w _ _ _

s l _ _ _

Draw lines to match.

bed

sled

wed

shed

Which word does not belong?
Fill in the bubble.

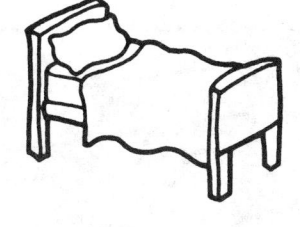

1. bed   red   bad
    ◯   ◯   ◯

2. fed   weed   wed
    ◯   ◯   ◯

3. lad   led   shed
    ◯   ◯   ◯

Draw a picture
of your favorite
-ed word.

Write words that end with -ell.

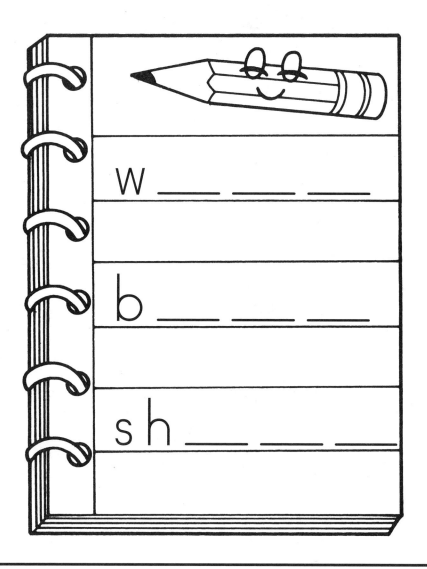

W _____

b _____

s h _____

Color each item that ends with -ell.

Name: _____

Draw lines to match.

well

shell

bell

spell

Which word does not belong?
Fill in the bubble.

1.   pull   tell   well
      ◯   ◯   ◯

2.   spell   spill   shell
      ◯   ◯   ◯

3.   fell   sell   fall
      ◯   ◯   ◯

Draw a picture
of your favorite
-ell word.

Write words that end with -en.

Color each item that ends with -en.

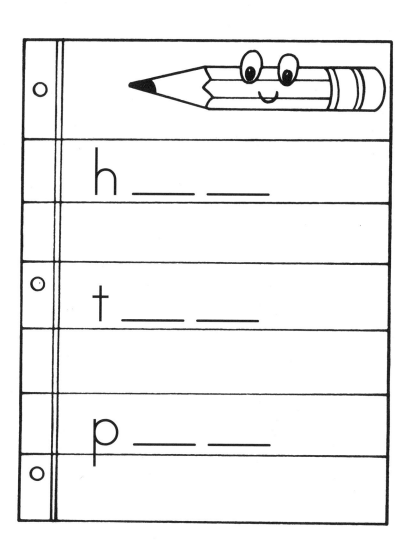

h _ _

t _ _

p _ _

10

Name: _____

Draw lines to match.

men

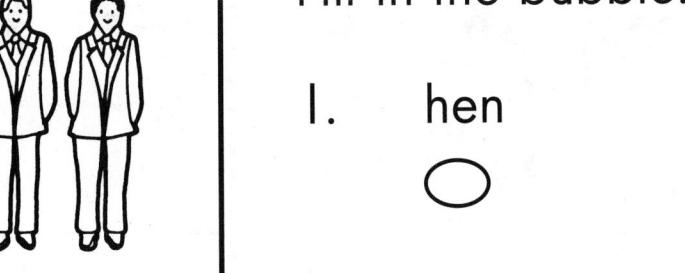

hen

10

ten

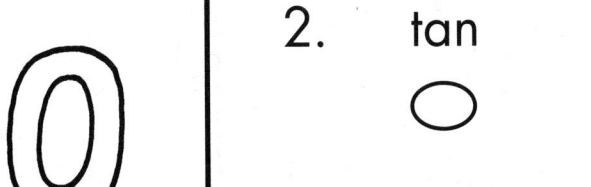

pen

Which word does not belong?
Fill in the bubble.

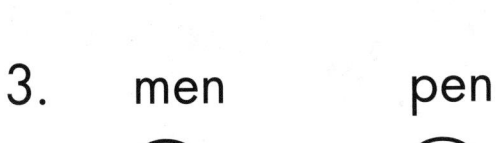

1. hen   hand   den
     ◯   ◯   ◯

2. tan   when   ten
     ◯   ◯   ◯

3. men   pen   pin
     ◯   ◯   ◯

Draw a picture
of your favorite
-en word.

☆ 17 ☆ Name: _____

Write words that end with **-est**.

Color each item that ends with **-est**.

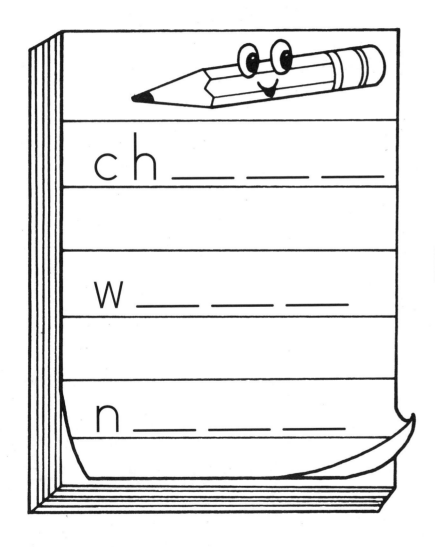

c h _ _ _ _ _

w _ _ _ _ _

n _ _ _ _ _

Draw lines to match.

west

vest

nest

chest

Which word does not belong?
Fill in the bubble.

1.   pest   mast   test
        ◯   ◯   ◯

2.   bust   nest   best
        ◯   ◯   ◯

3.   rest   chest   rent
        ◯   ◯   ◯

Draw a picture
of your favorite
-est word.

Write words that end with -et.

Color each item that ends with -et.

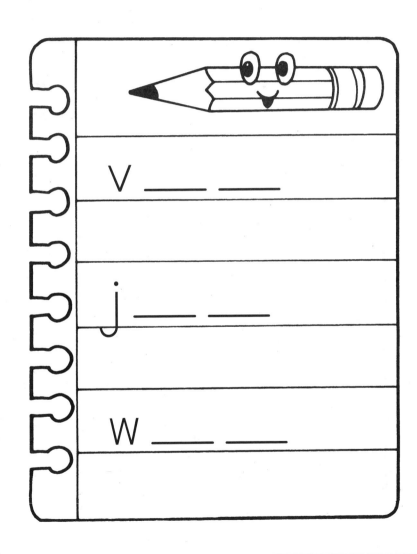

V _ _ _

j _ _ _

W _ _ _

Draw lines to match.

wet

vet

jet

net

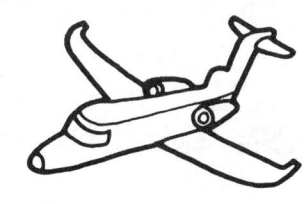

Which word does not belong? Fill in the bubble.

1.   sat   let   net
     ◯   ◯   ◯

2.   get   yet   got
     ◯   ◯   ◯

3.   wet   pat   pet
     ◯   ◯   ◯

Draw a picture of your favorite **-et** word.

Write words that end with -ick.

Color each item that ends with -ick.

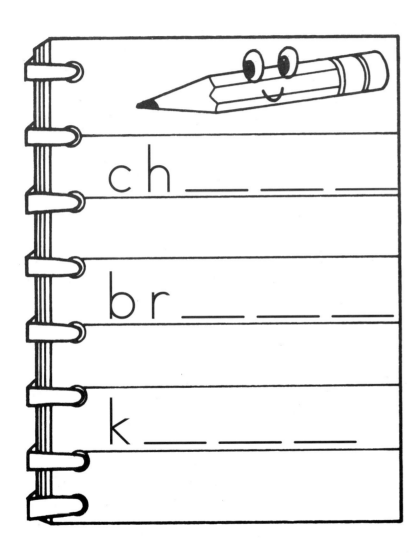

c h _ _ _ _ _

b r _ _ _ _ _

k _ _ _ _ _

Name: _____

Draw lines to match.

brick

kick

chick

stick

Which word does not belong?
Fill in the bubble.

1. pick   trick   pig
    ◯   ◯   ◯

2. sick   chin   chick
    ◯   ◯   ◯

3. tock   stick   tick
    ◯   ◯   ◯

Draw a picture
of your favorite
-ick word.

Name: _____

Write words that end with **-ig**.

Color each item that ends with **-ig**.

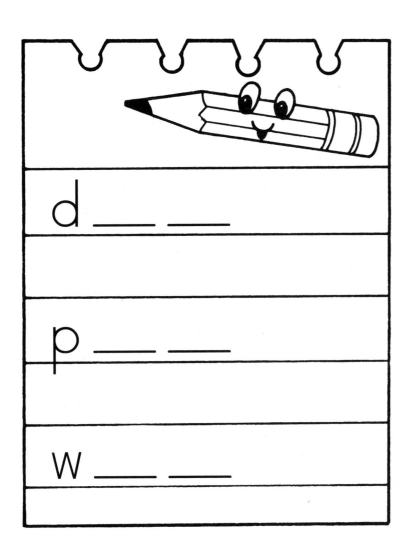

d _ _ _

p _ _ _

W _ _ _

Draw lines to match.

twig

dig

pig

wig

Which word does not belong? Fill in the bubble.

1.   pig   kick   big
     ◯   ◯   ◯

2.   get   fig   twig
     ◯   ◯   ◯

3.   wig   dig   wick
     ◯   ◯   ◯

Draw a picture of your favorite **-ig** word.

Name: _____

Write words that end with -**in**.

Color each item that ends with -**in**.

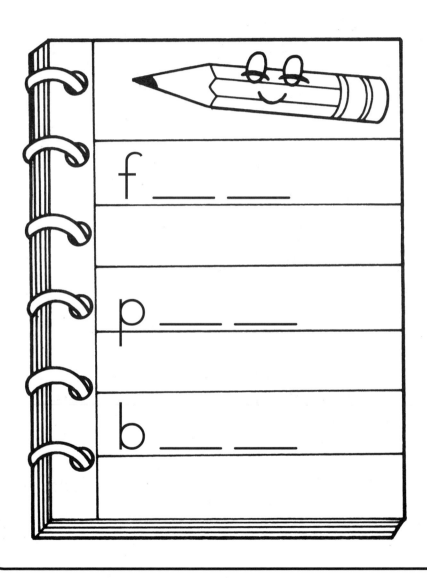

f _ _ _

p _ _ _

b _ _ _

 26   Name: _____

Draw lines to match.

chin

pin

bin

fin

Which word does not belong? Fill in the bubble.

1.   fine   win   grin
      ◯   ◯   ◯

2.   spin   fin   find
      ◯   ◯   ◯

3.   tin   pine   pin
      ◯   ◯   ◯

Draw a picture
of your favorite
-in word.

Name: _____

Write words that end with -**ing**.

Color each item that ends with -**ing**.

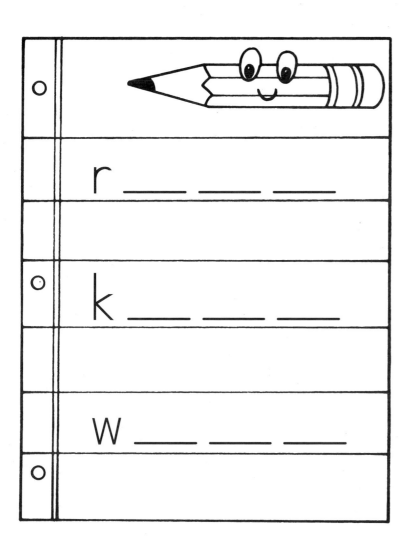

r _ _ _ _ _

k _ _ _ _ _

W _ _ _ _ _

Name: _____

Draw lines to match.

sing

king

ring

swing

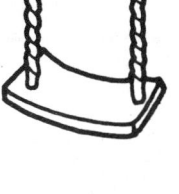

Which word does not belong?
Fill in the bubble.

1. thing   pink   king
   ◯   ◯   ◯

2. stick   sting   sing
   ◯   ◯   ◯

3. wing   ring   win
   ◯   ◯   ◯

Draw a picture
of your favorite
-ing word.

Write words that end with -it.

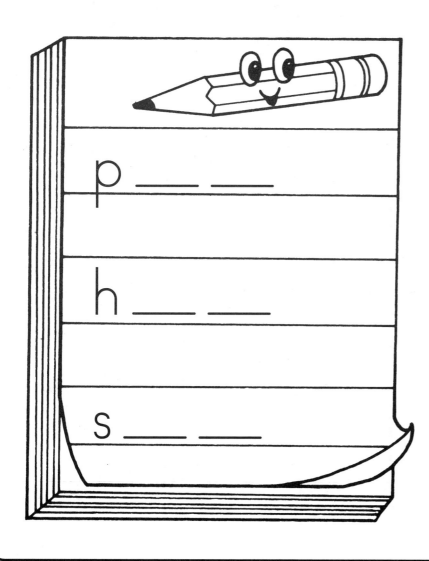

p _ _ _

h _ _ _

s _ _ _

Color each item that ends with -it.

Draw lines to match.

knit

hit

pit

sit

Which word does not belong?
Fill in the bubble.

1.   fit   sit   fin
    ◯   ◯   ◯

2.   kit   kid   hit
    ◯   ◯   ◯

3.   bite   bit   knit
    ◯   ◯   ◯

Draw a picture
of your favorite
-it word.

Write words that end with -ock.

Color each item that ends with -ock.

c l _ _ _ _ _

l _ _ _ _ _

s _ _ _ _ _

Name: _____

Draw lines to match.

clock

lock

block

sock

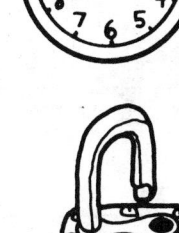

Which word does not belong?
Fill in the bubble.

1. soak   knock   sock
   ◯   ◯   ◯

2. rock   lock   look
   ◯   ◯   ◯

3. dock   float   flock
   ◯   ◯   ◯

Draw a picture
of your favorite
-ock word.

Write words that end with **-og**.

Color each item that ends with **-og**.

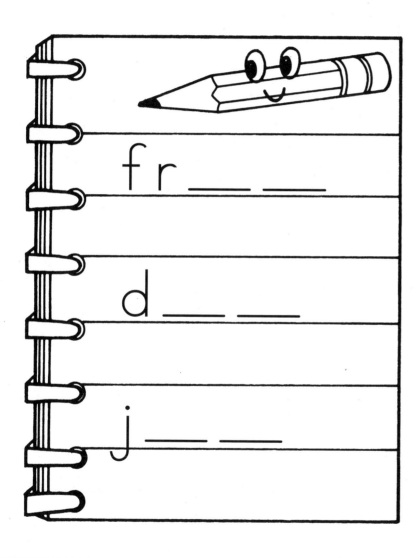

f r ____ ____

d ____ ____

j ____ ____

Draw lines to match.

log

frog

dog

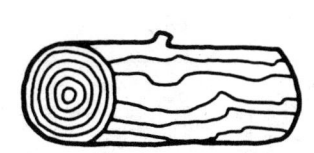

jog

Which word does not belong?
Fill in the bubble.

1.   hog   lock   log
      ◯   ◯   ◯

2.   bag   bog   smog
      ◯   ◯   ◯

3.   dog   jog   pig
      ◯   ◯   ◯

Draw a picture
of your favorite
-og word.

Write words that end with **-op**.

Color each item that ends with **-op**.

t _ _

m _ _ _

s t _ _ _

Draw lines to match.

top

hop

stop

mop

Which word does not belong? Fill in the bubble.

1.   pop   drop   pod
     ◯   ◯   ◯

2.   chop   hot   hop
     ◯   ◯   ◯

3.   map   top   mop
     ◯   ◯   ◯

Draw a picture of your favorite **-op** word.

Write words that end with -ot.

Color each item that ends with -ot.

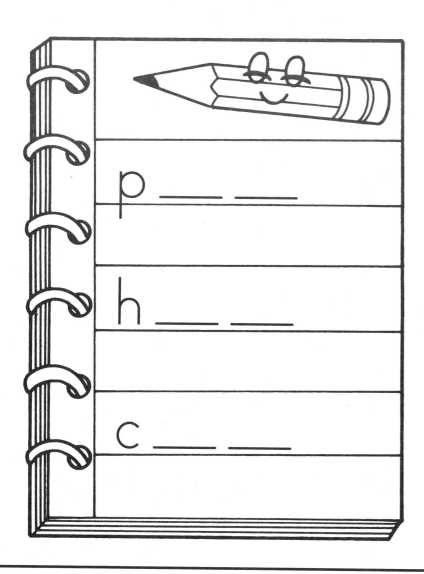

p _ _ _

h _ _ _

c _ _ _

☆38☆ Name: _____

Draw lines to match.

pot

hot

cot

knot

Which word does not belong?
Fill in the bubble.

1. dot   hat   hot
   ◯   ◯   ◯

2. pet   slot   pot
   ◯   ◯   ◯

3. knot   got   goat
   ◯   ◯   ◯

Draw a picture
of your favorite
-ot word.

Write words that end with -uck.

Color each item that ends with -uck.

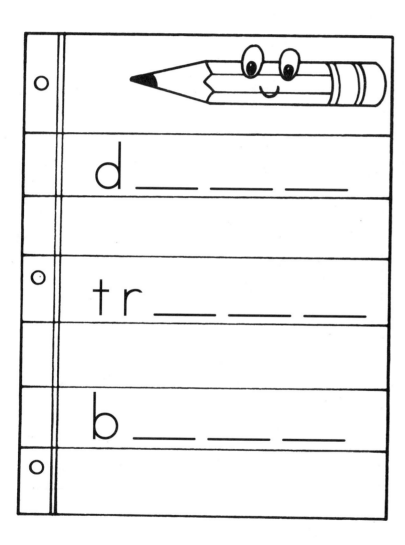

d _____

tr _____

b _____

40 Name: _____

Draw lines to match.

duck

stuck

truck

buck

Which word does not belong? Fill in the bubble.

1. pack ○   luck ○   puck ○

2. tick ○   tuck ○   duck ○

3. muck ○   back ○   buck ○

Draw a picture of your favorite **-uck** word.

Write words that end with -**ug**.

Color each item that ends with -**ug**.

r _ _ _

p l _ _ _

m _ _ _

Draw lines to match.

rug

mug

plug

bug

Which word does not belong? Fill in the bubble.

1.   dug   dog   hug
     ○   ○   ○

2.   red   rug   tug
     ○   ○   ○

3.   bug   jug   jog
     ○   ○   ○

Draw a picture
of your favorite
-ug word.

Write words that end with -**ump**.

Color each item that ends with -**ump**.

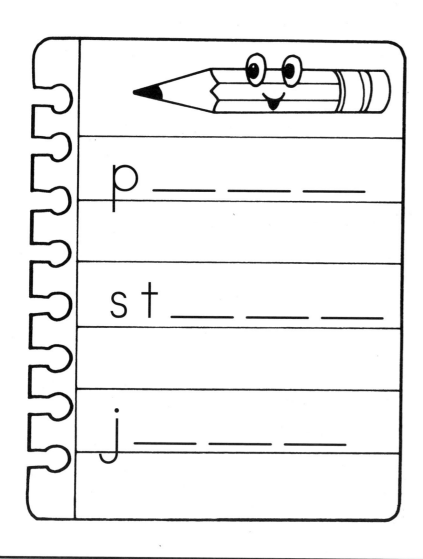

p _____

s t _____

j _____

**44**   Name: _____

Draw lines to match.

dump

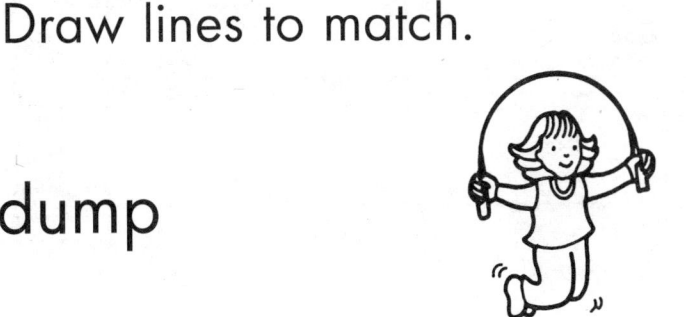

stump

pump

jump

Which word does not belong? Fill in the bubble.

1.   drum   bump   lump
     ⬭   ⬭   ⬭

2.   hump   dump   down
     ⬭   ⬭   ⬭

3.   jump   job   pump
     ⬭   ⬭   ⬭

Draw a picture
of your favorite
-ump word.

Write words that end with -**unk**.

Color each item that ends with -**unk**.

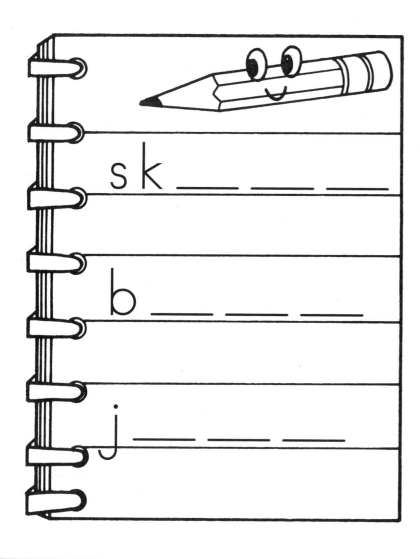

s k _ _ _ _ _ _ _

b _ _ _ _ _ _ _

j _ _ _ _ _ _ _

Draw lines to match.

skunk

junk

trunk

bunk

Which word does not belong? Fill in the bubble.

1. dunk   dark   skunk
    ◯   ◯   ◯

2. honk   hunk   chunk
    ◯   ◯   ◯

3. spunk   junk   spark
    ◯   ◯   ◯

Draw a picture of your favorite **-unk** word.

Name: _____

Write words that end with -**ake**.

Color each item that ends with -**ake**.

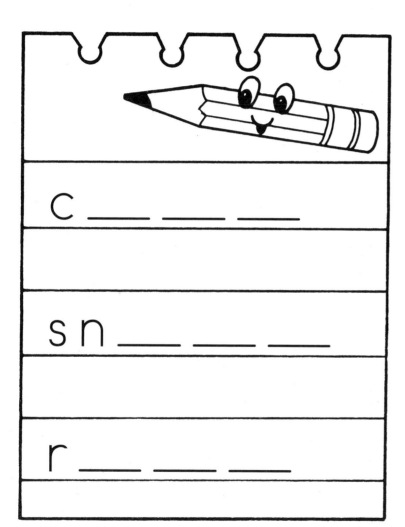

c _ _ _ _ _

s n _ _ _ _ _

r _ _ _ _ _

Name: _____

Draw lines to match.

lake

rake

snake

cake

Which word does not belong?
Fill in the bubble.

1. make   talk   take
    ⭕   ⭕   ⭕

2. snack   snake   fake
    ⭕   ⭕   ⭕

3. bake   lake   back
    ⭕   ⭕   ⭕

Draw a picture
of your favorite
-ake word.

Write words that end with **-ale**.

Color each item that ends with **-ale**.

w h _____

s _____

b _____

$10.00

NOW $5.00

Draw lines to match.

whale

sale

scale

bale

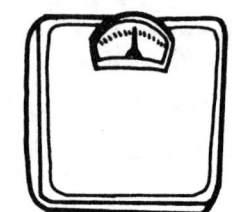

Which word does not belong?
Fill in the bubble.

1.   pale   pole   bale
      ○   ○   ○

2.   whale   stale   whole
      ○   ○   ○

3.   male   tall   tale
      ○   ○   ○

Draw a picture
of your favorite
-ale word.

Write words that end with -**ame**.

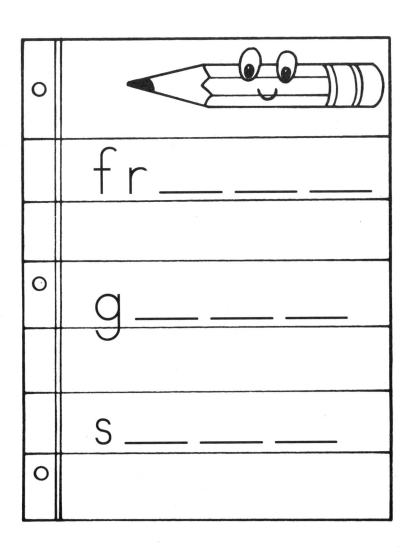

fr _ _ _ _ _

g _ _ _ _ _

s _ _ _ _ _

Color each item that ends with -**ame**.

Draw lines to match.

game

frame

same

flame

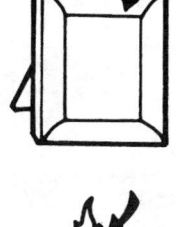

Which word does not belong?
Fill in the bubble.

1. came   same   come
   ◯   ◯   ◯

2. tame   time   lame
   ◯   ◯   ◯

3. fan   blame   fame
   ◯   ◯   ◯

Draw a picture
of your favorite
-ame word.

Name: _____

Write words that end with **-ice**.

Color each item that ends with **-ice**.

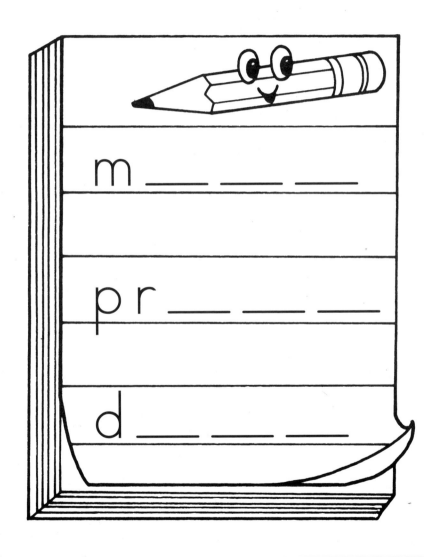

m _____

p r _____

d _____

$5.00

Draw lines to match.

price

ice

mice

dice

Which word does not belong?
Fill in the bubble.

1.   slice   slide   dice
     ○   ○   ○

2.   mice   spice   mine
     ○   ○   ○

3.   twice   right   rice
     ○   ○   ○

Draw a picture
of your favorite
-ice word.

Name: _____

Write words that end with **-ide**.

Color each item that ends with **-ide**.

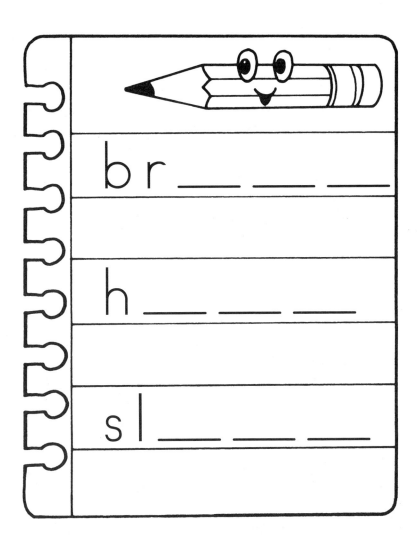

b r _ _ _ _ _

h _ _ _ _ _

s l _ _ _ _ _

Draw lines to match.

ride

bride

hide

slide

Which word does not belong?
Fill in the bubble.

1. ride   nine   hide
    ◯   ◯   ◯

2. dive   side   wide
    ◯   ◯   ◯

3. tide   glide   time
    ◯   ◯   ◯

Draw a picture
of your favorite
-ide word.

Name: _____

Write words that end with **-ine**.

Color each item that ends with **-ine**.

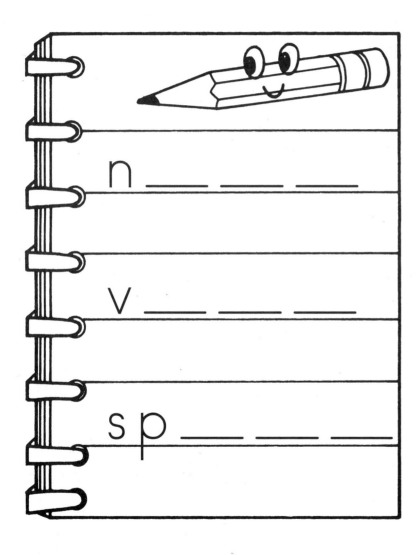

n _____

v _____

s p _____

 58 Name: _____

Draw lines to match.

vine

nine

line

spine

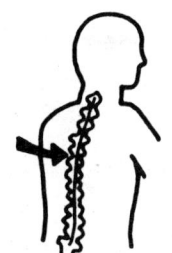

Which word does not belong?
Fill in the bubble.

1. dime   dine   spine
    ⬭   ⬭   ⬭

2. pine   mine   pin
    ⬭   ⬭   ⬭

3. fine   tie   twine
    ⬭   ⬭   ⬭

Draw a picture
of your favorite
-ine word.

Name: _____

Write words that end with -**ole**.

Color each item that ends with -**ole**.

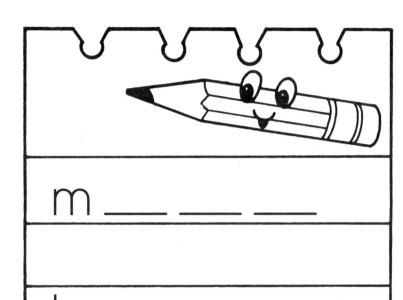

m _ _ _ _

h _ _ _ _

p _ _ _ _

Word Family: -ole

Draw lines to match.

pole

mole

hole

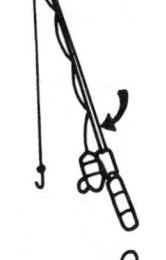

tadpole

Which word does not belong? Fill in the bubble.

1. whole   role   wall
    ◯   ◯   ◯

2. stole   stale   pole
    ◯   ◯   ◯

3. mile   mole   hole
    ◯   ◯   ◯

Draw a picture
of your favorite
-ole word.

Name: _____

Write words that end with **-one**.

Color each item that ends with **-one**.

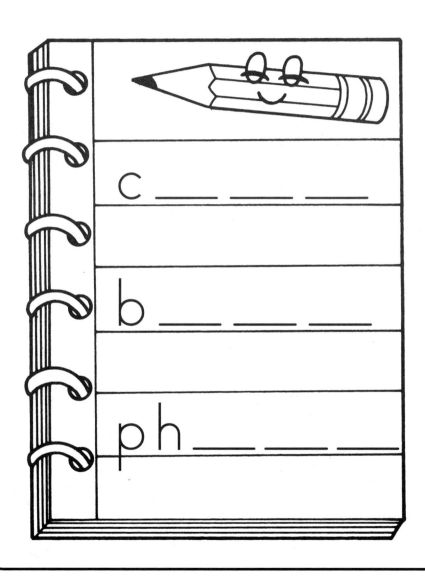

c _ _ _ _ _ _

b _ _ _ _ _ _

p h _ _ _ _ _

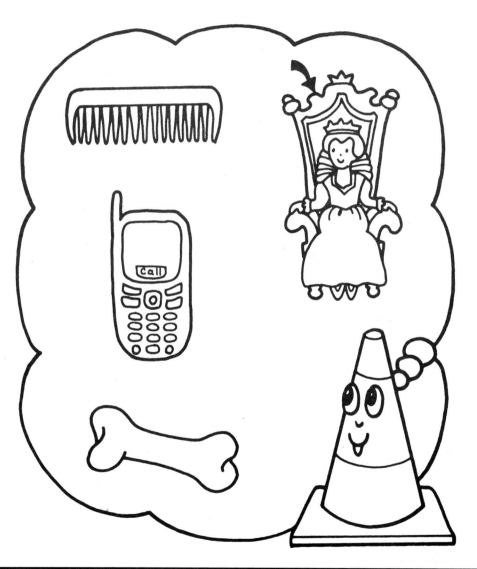

 62 Name: _____

Draw lines to match.

bone

throne

cone

phone

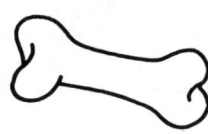

Which word does not belong? Fill in the bubble.

1. lawn ◯   lone ◯   tone ◯

2. bone ◯   phone ◯   bun ◯

3. cone ◯   come ◯   throne ◯

Draw a picture of your favorite **-one** word.

Write words that end with -**ose**.

Color each item that ends with -**ose**.

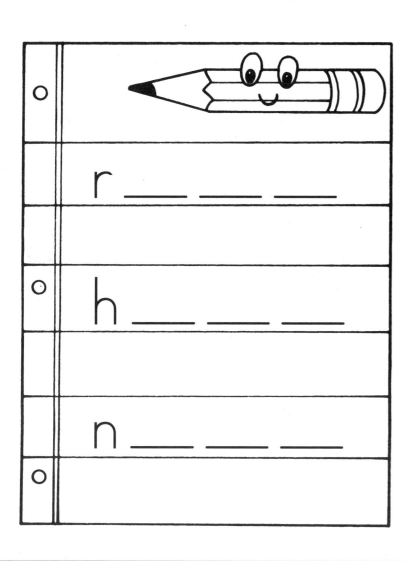

r _ _ _ _ _

h _ _ _ _ _

n _ _ _ _ _

Name: _____

Draw lines to match.

nose

rose

close

hose

Which word does not belong? Fill in the bubble.

1. those   note   nose
   ○   ○   ○

2. pass   pose   rose
   ○   ○   ○

3. hose   close   claws
   ○   ○   ○

Draw a picture
of your favorite
-ose word.

Write words that end with -**ail**.

Color each item that ends with -**ail**.

t _____

p _____

s _____

Name: _____

Draw lines to match.

sail

pail

nail

snail

Which word does not belong? Fill in the bubble.

1. nail ⬭   maid ⬭   mail ⬭

2. trail ⬭   rail ⬭   rain ⬭

3. pain ⬭   bail ⬭   sail ⬭

Draw a picture of your favorite **-ail** word.

Name: _____

Write words that end with -**ain**.

Color each item that ends with -**ain**.

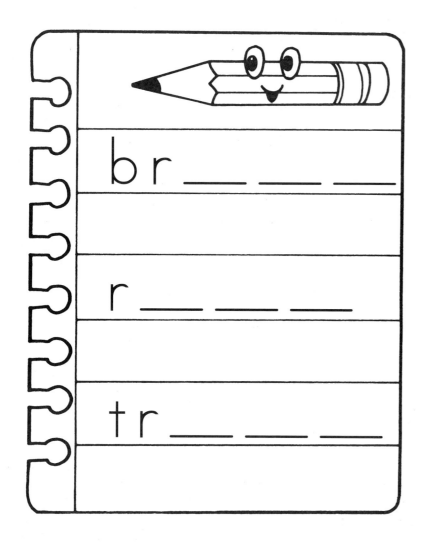

b r _ _ _ _

r _ _ _ _

t r _ _ _ _

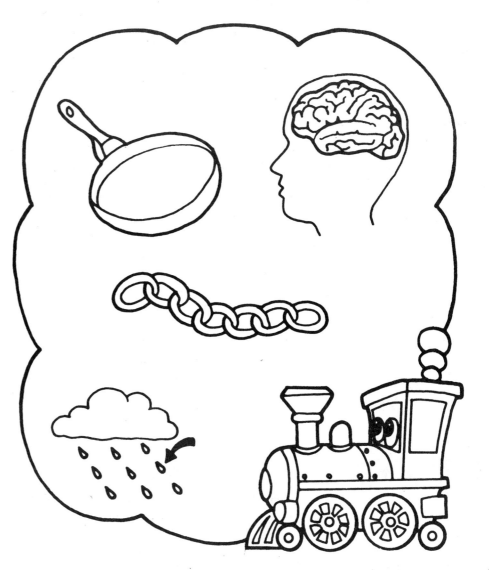

Name: _____

Draw lines to match.

chain

rain

train

brain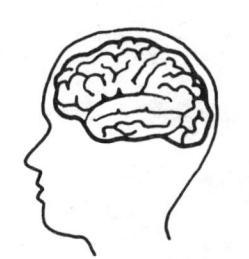

Which word does not belong?
Fill in the bubble.

1. stain   pain   star
    ◯   ◯   ◯

2. main   maid   train
    ◯   ◯   ◯

3. raid   rain   drain
    ◯   ◯   ◯

Draw a picture
of your favorite
-ain word.

Name: _____

Word Family: -ay

Write words that end with **-ay**.

Color each item that ends with **-ay**.

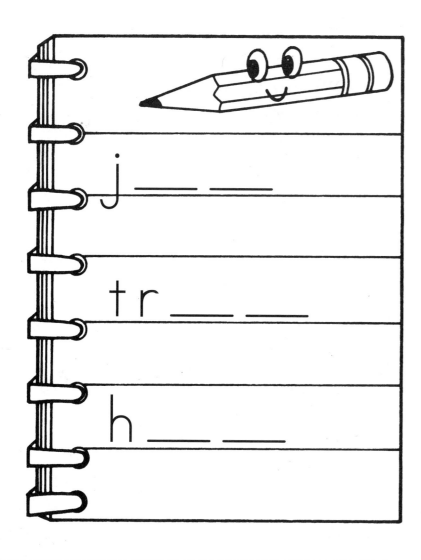

j _ _ _ _

t r _ _ _ _

h _ _ _ _

Draw lines to match.

tray

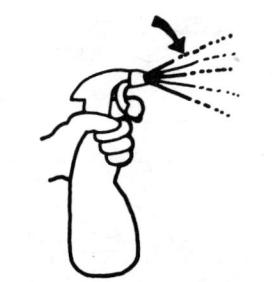

hay

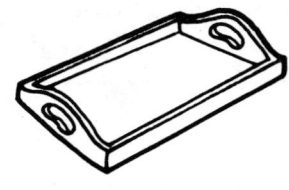

spray

jay

Which word does not belong?
Fill in the bubble.

1.   pain   day   pay
     ○   ○   ○

2.   clay   may   claw
     ○   ○   ○

3.   bay   trail   tray
     ○   ○   ○

Draw a picture
of your favorite
-ay word.

Name: _____

Write words that end with -**eat**.

s _____

w h _____

m _____

Color each item that ends with -**eat**.

Name: _____

Draw lines to match.

heat

wheat

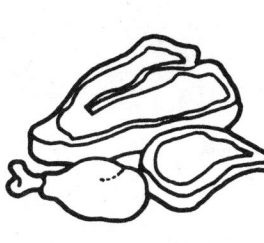

seat

meat

Which word does not belong?
Fill in the bubble.

1. meat   team   treat
    ⬭   ⬭   ⬭

2. heal   heat   beat
    ⬭   ⬭   ⬭

3. seat   wheat   seam
    ⬭   ⬭   ⬭

Draw a picture
of your favorite
-eat word.

Name: _____

Write words that end with -ee.

Color each item that ends with -ee.

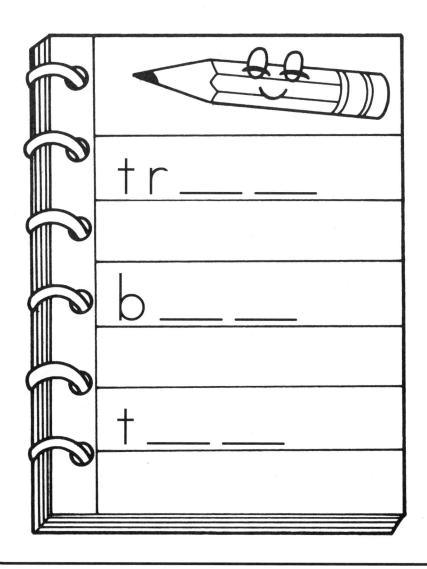

tr_____

b_____

t_____

3

Name: _____

Draw lines to match.

tee

bee

tree

three

3

Which word does not belong?
Fill in the bubble.

1. knee   see   week
    ◯   ◯   ◯

2. free   feed   tee
    ◯   ◯   ◯

3. need   bee   three
    ◯   ◯   ◯

Draw a picture
of your favorite
-ee word.

Write words that end with -eel.

Color each item that ends with -eel.

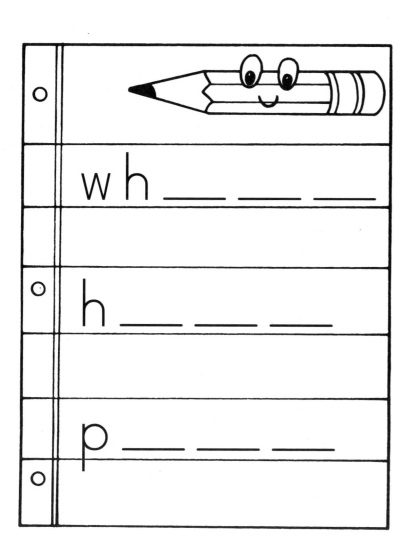

w h _____

h _____

p _____

Name: _____

Draw lines to match.

peel

heel

eel

wheel

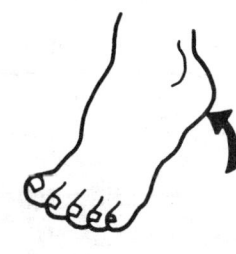

Which word does not belong?
Fill in the bubble.

1. fell   feel   heel
    ○   ○   ○

2. kneel   reel   read
    ○   ○   ○

3. eel   bell   wheel
    ○   ○   ○

Draw a picture
of your favorite
-eel word.

Write words that end with -**eet**.

Color each item that ends with -**eet**.

b _____

f _____

m _____

Draw lines to match.

feet

street

beet

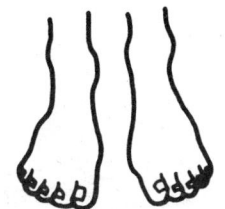

meet

Which word does not belong?
Fill in the bubble.

1. sheet   sheep   greet
    ○   ○   ○

2. bean   tweet   beet
    ○   ○   ○

3. sweet   street   tree
    ○   ○   ○

Draw a picture
of your favorite
-eet word.

Write words that end with -**ight**.

Color each item that ends with -**ight**.

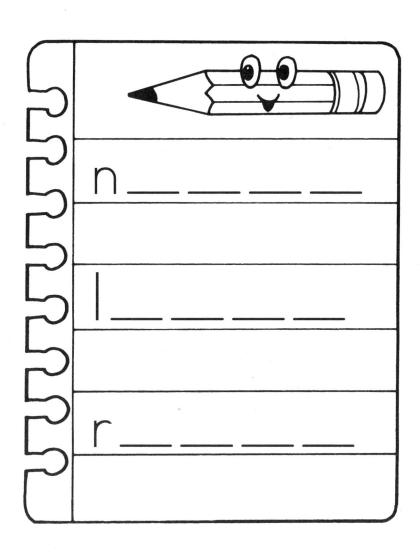

n _ _ _ _ _ _

l _ _ _ _ _

r _ _ _ _ _ _

Draw lines to match.

night

right

light

knight

Which word does not belong?
Fill in the bubble.

1.   fight   right   rent
     ○   ○   ○

2.   bright   sting   tight
     ○   ○   ○

3.   mint   might   night
     ○   ○   ○

Draw a picture
of your favorite
-ight word.

Name: _____

Write words that end with -oat.

Color each item that ends with -oat.

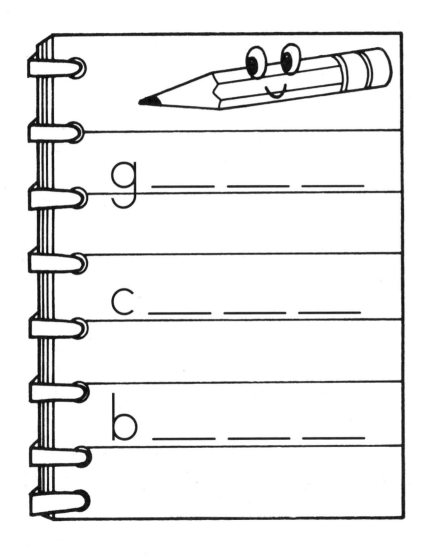

g _____

c _____

b _____

Name: _____

Draw lines to match.

goat

coat

boat

float

Which word does not belong?
Fill in the bubble.

1. float   flat   boat
    ◯   ◯   ◯

2. soap   moat   oat
    ◯   ◯   ◯

3. throat   goat   got
    ◯   ◯   ◯

Draw a picture
of your favorite
-oat word.

Write words that end with -ow.

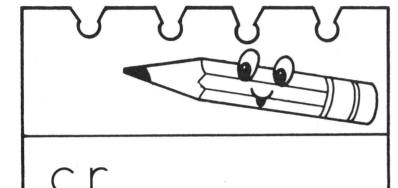

c r ___ ___ ___

b ___ ___ ___

r ___ ___ ___

Color each item that ends with -ow.

Name: _____

Draw lines to match.

snow

row

crow

bow

Which word does not belong? Fill in the bubble.

1. low   gown   grow
    ○   ○   ○

2. now   snow   mow
    ○   ○   ○

3. throw   blow   throne
    ○   ○   ○

Draw a picture
of your favorite
-ow word.

Write words that end with -all.

Color each item that ends with -all.

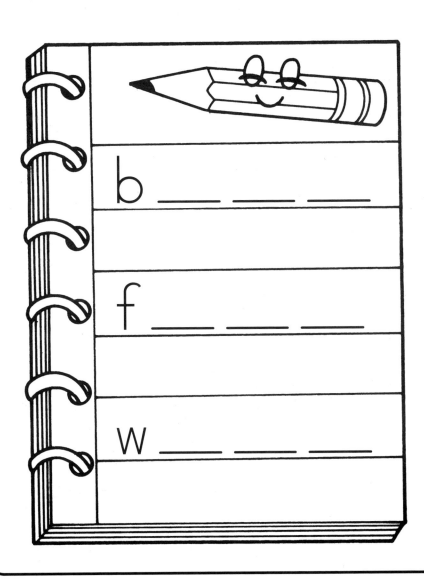

b _____

f _____

W _____

Name: _____

Draw lines to match.

tall

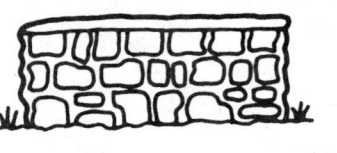

ball

wall

fall

Which word does not belong?
Fill in the bubble.

1. small   smell   call
    ○   ○   ○

2. ball   mall   mail
    ○   ○   ○

3. hall   tale   tall
    ○   ○   ○

Draw a picture
of your favorite
-all word.

Name: _____

Write words that end with -aw.

Color each item that ends with -aw.

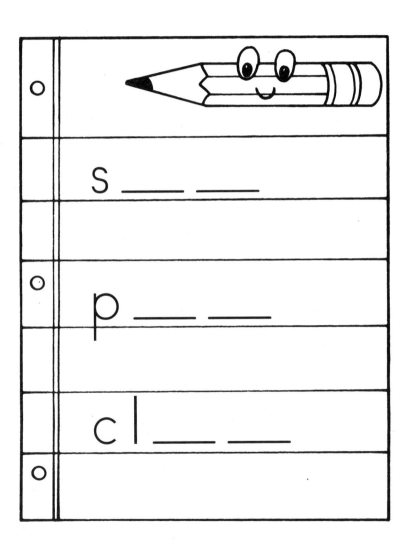

s _____

p _____

c l _____

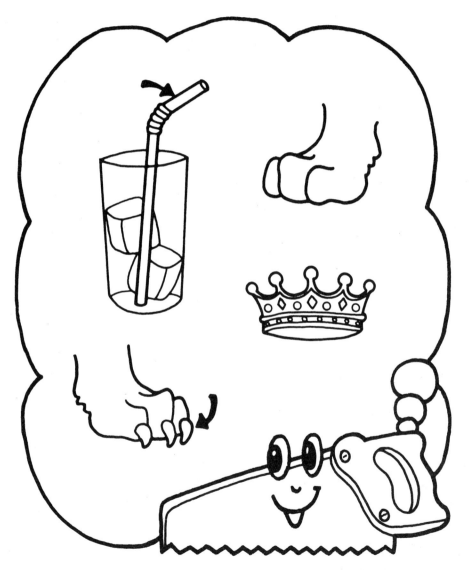

Draw lines to match.

paw

straw

saw

claw

Which word does not belong? Fill in the bubble.

1.   jaw   claw   jam
     ⬭   ⬭   ⬭

2.   law   lawn   saw
     ⬭   ⬭   ⬭

3.   star   raw   straw
     ⬭   ⬭   ⬭

Draw a picture
of your favorite
-aw word.

Write words that end with -**ook**.   Color each item that ends with -**ook**.

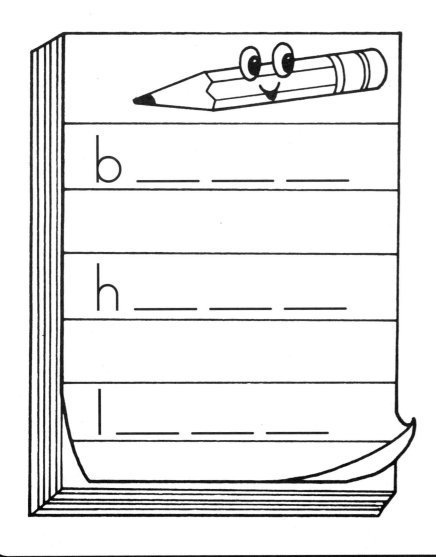

b _ _ _ _ _ _

h _ _ _ _ _ _

l _ _ _ _ _ _

Draw lines to match.

cook

hook

book

look

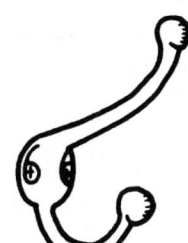

Which word does not belong?
Fill in the bubble.

1. knock   nook   brook
    ◯   ◯   ◯

2. took   shook   talk
    ◯   ◯   ◯

3. crook   crack   hook
    ◯   ◯   ◯

Draw a picture
of your favorite
-**ook** word.

Name: _____

Write words that end with -**ool**.

Color each item that ends with -**ool**.

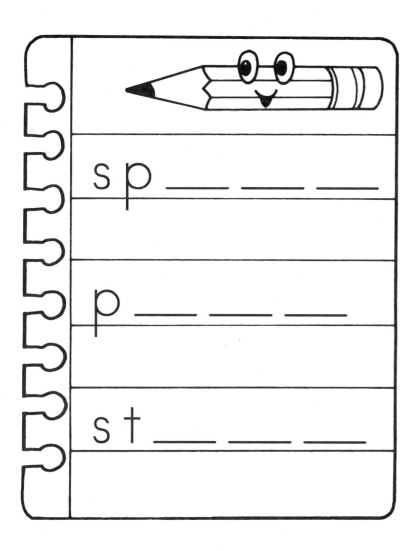

s p _ _ _ _ _

p _ _ _ _ _

s t _ _ _ _ _

Draw lines to match.

school

pool

stool

spool

Which word does not belong?
Fill in the bubble.

1.   fool   foul   stool
     ◯   ◯   ◯

2.   tool   pool   tall
     ◯   ◯   ◯

3.   cool   doll   drool
     ◯   ◯   ◯

Draw a picture
of your favorite
-ool word.

Write words that end with -**oot**.

Color each item that ends with -**oot**.

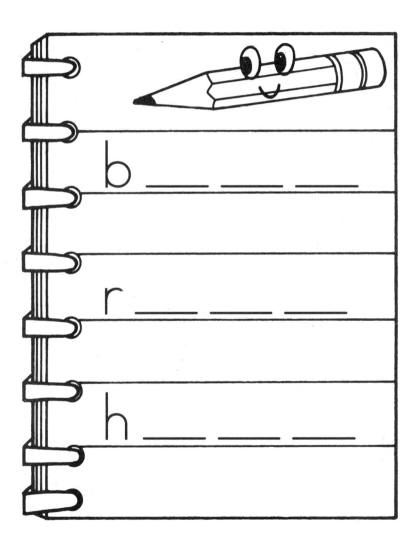

b _ _ _ _

r _ _ _ _

h _ _ _ _

Whoo

Name: _____

Draw lines to match.

toot

boot

root

hoot

Which word does not belong?
Fill in the bubble.

1.　shoot　　root　　shot
　　 ○　　　　○　　　　○

2.　hoot　　hot　　loot
　　 ○　　　　○　　　　○

3.　toad　　scoot　　toot
　　 ○　　　　○　　　　○

Draw a picture
of your favorite
-oot word.

Name: _____

Write words that end with -**oil**.

Color each item that ends with -**oil**.

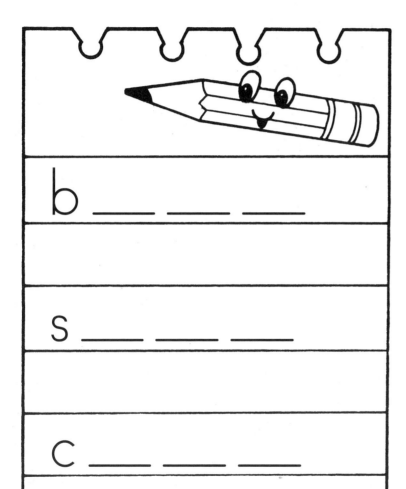

b _____ _____ _____ _____

s _____ _____ _____ _____

c _____ _____ _____ _____

Good Garden

Name: _____

Draw lines to match.

soil

oil

boil

coil

Which word does not belong?
Fill in the bubble.

1.   call   foil   coil
     ◯   ◯   ◯

2.   boil   toil   tail
     ◯   ◯   ◯

3.   soil   all   oil
     ◯   ◯   ◯

Draw a picture
of your favorite
-**oil** word.

Write words that end with -**own**.   Color each item that ends with -**own**.

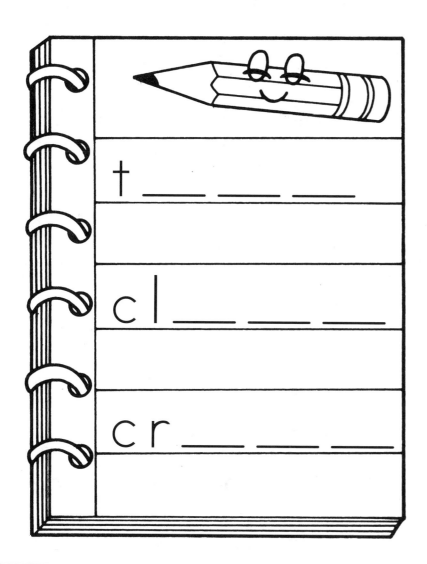

t _ _ _ _

c l _ _ _ _

c r _ _ _ _

Name: _____

Draw lines to match.

clown

town

frown

crown

Which word does not belong?
Fill in the bubble.

1. brown   yawn   crown
    ◯   ◯   ◯

2. our   town   down
    ◯   ◯   ◯

3. frown   clown   claw
    ◯   ◯   ◯

Draw a picture
of your favorite
-own word.

Write words that end with -ar.

Color each item that ends with -ar.

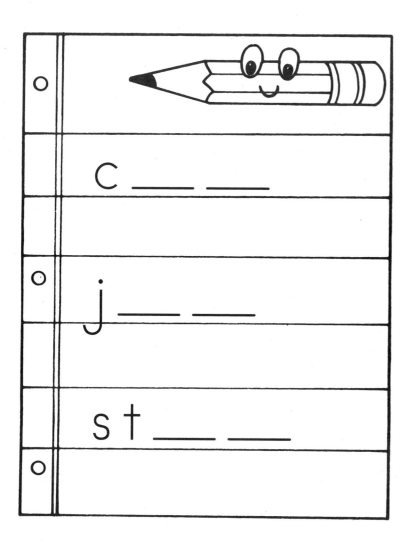

C _ _ _

j _ _ _

s t _ _ _

Name: _____

Draw lines to match.

star

jar

bar

car

Which word does not belong?
Fill in the bubble.

1. tar   tan   bar
    ○   ○   ○

2. far   car   care
    ○   ○   ○

3. jar   tear   scar
    ○   ○   ○

Draw a picture
of your favorite
-ar word.

Write words that end with **-ore**.

Color each item that ends with **-ore**.

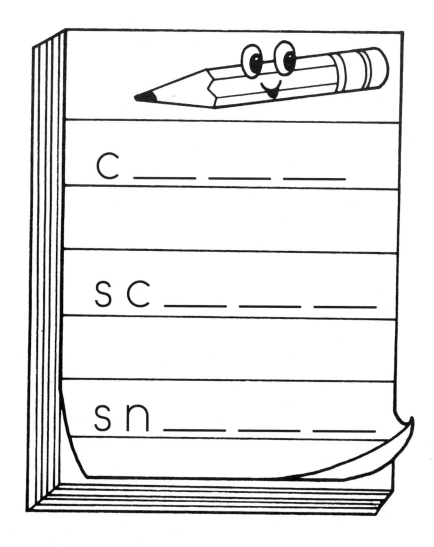

c _____ _____ _____

s c _____ _____ _____

s n _____ _____

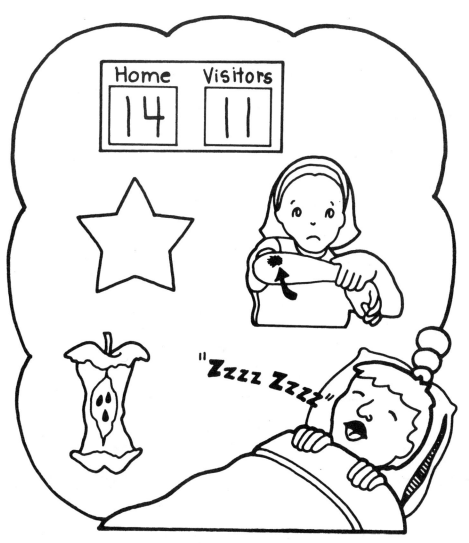

Home   Visitors

14   11

"Zzzz Zzzz"

Draw lines to match.

core

snore

score

sore

Which word does not belong?
Fill in the bubble.

1.   bore   more   bar
     ○   ○   ○

2.   pore   pole   tore
     ○   ○   ○

3.   phone   chore   wore
     ○   ○   ○

Draw a picture
of your favorite
-**ore** word.

Name: _____

Write words that end with -**orn**.   Color each item that ends with -**orn**.

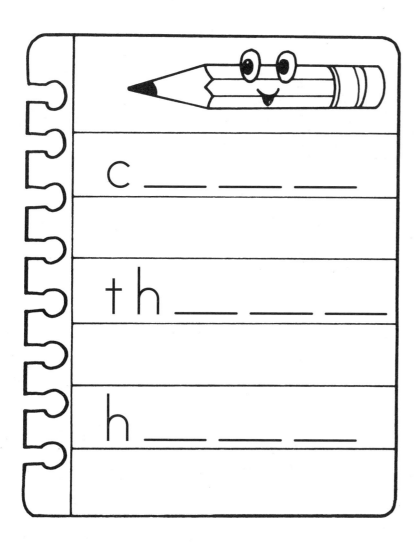

c _ _ _ _ _

t h _ _ _ _

h _ _ _ _

4

Name: _____

Draw lines to match.

horn

corn

thorn

acorn

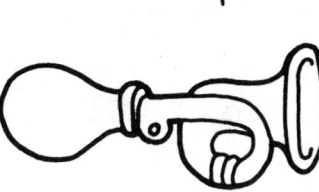
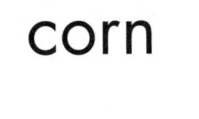

Which word does not belong? Fill in the bubble.

1. torn   barn   born
    ○   ○   ○

2. won   worn   thorn
    ○   ○   ○

3. morn   corn   more
    ○   ○   ○

Draw a picture of your favorite **-orn** word.

Name: _____

Trace.

Write **all**.

Find each **all**. Color that space red.
Then color the rest of the picture.

Name: _____

Trace.

am

am

am

Write **am**.

Find each **am**. Color that leaf orange. Then color the rest of the picture.

an

am

and

am

am

at

an

am

Trace.

and

and

and

Write **and**.

Find each **and**. Color that space green. Then color the rest of the picture.

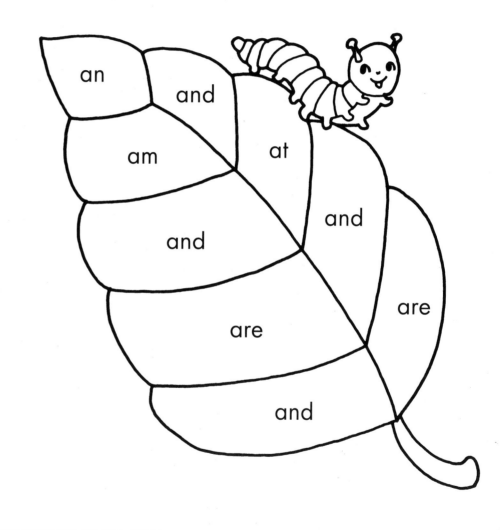

Name: _____

Trace.

are

are

are

Write **are**.

_____

Find each **are**. Color that star yellow. Then color the rest of the picture.

air

am

are

arm

are

art

are

are

Name: _____

Trace.

as

as

as

Write **as**.

_ _ _ _ _ _ _ _ _ _ _ _

Find each **as**. Color that space purple. Then color the rest of the picture.

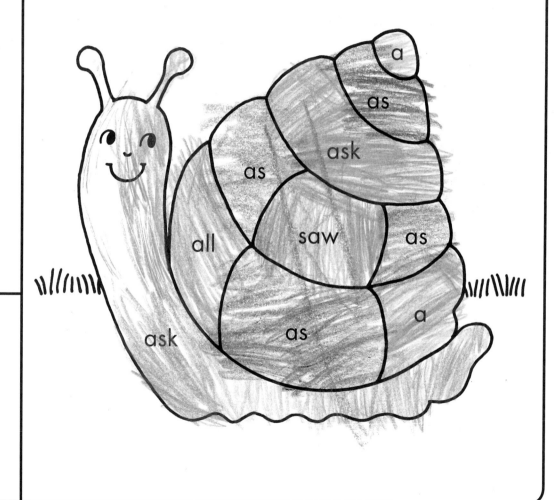

110 Name: ____________________

Sight Word: ask

Trace.

ask

ask

ask

Write **ask**.

Find each **ask**. Color that fish orange.
Then color the rest of the picture.

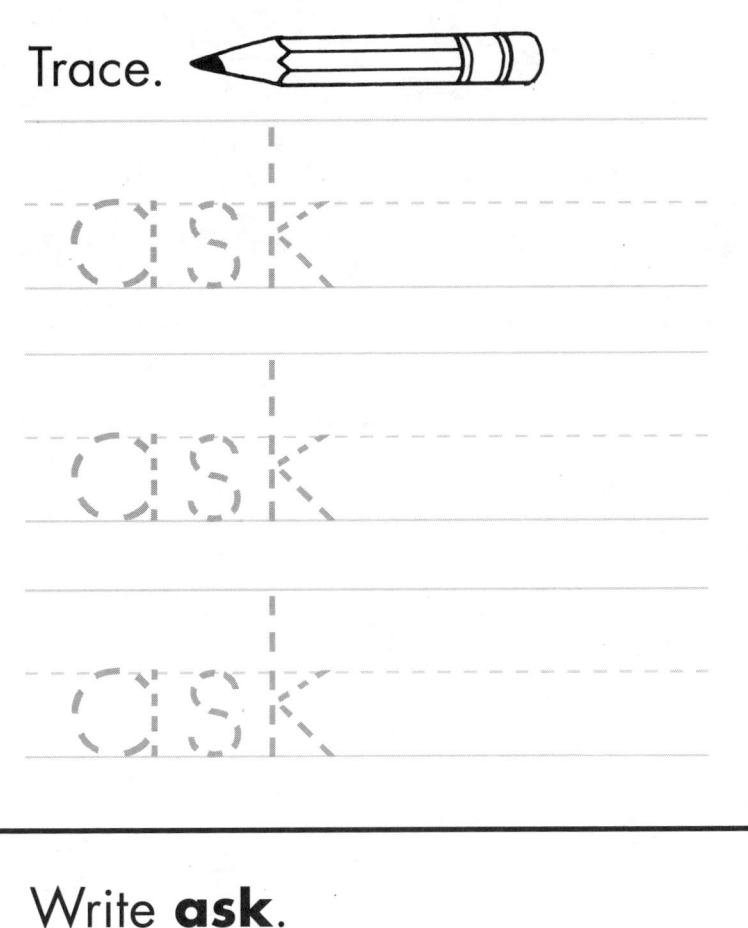

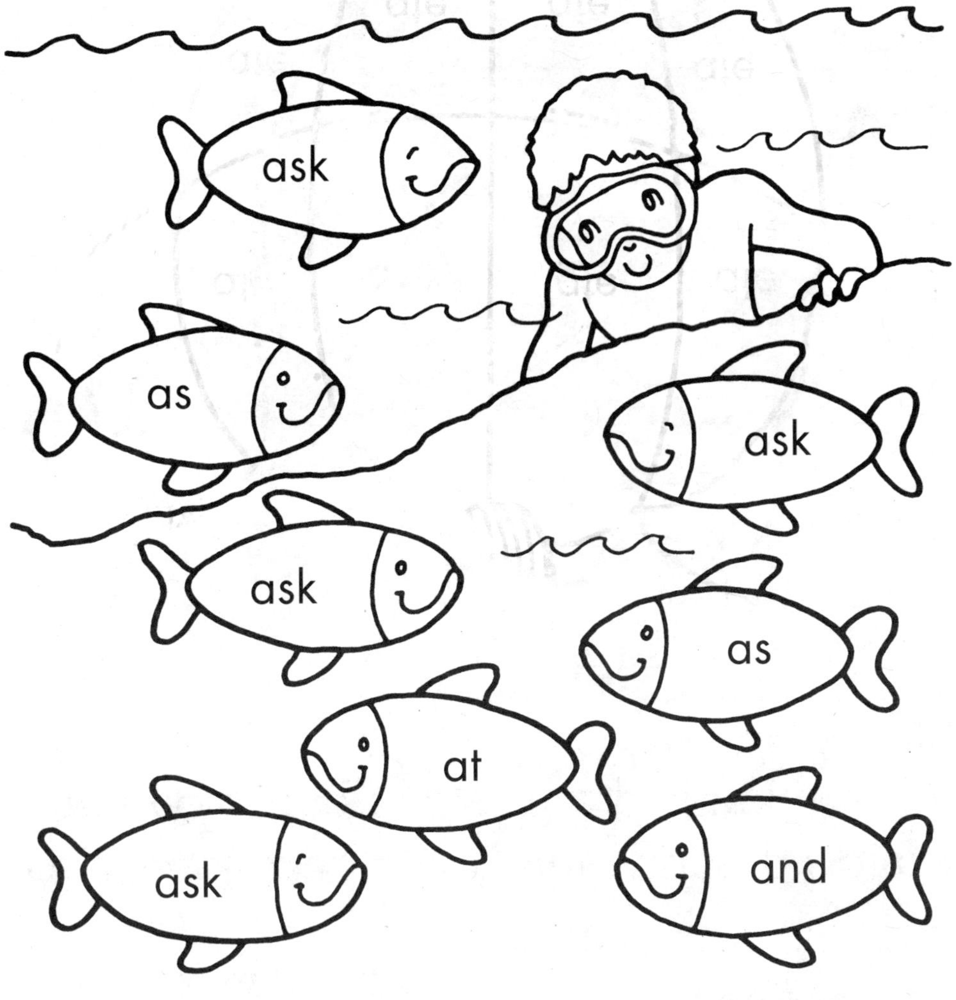

Name: _____

Trace.

Write **ate**.

_____

Find each **ate**. Color that space orange. Then color the rest of the picture.

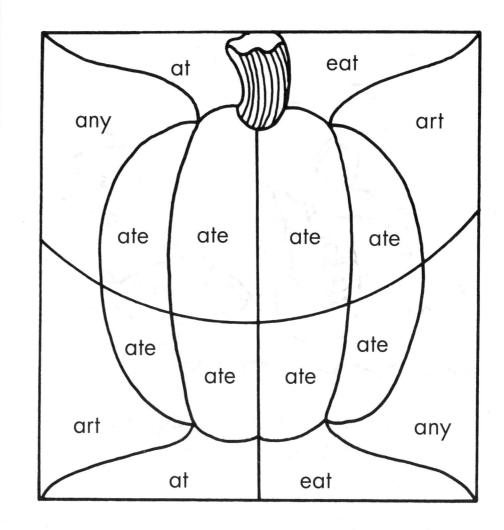

Name: _____

Trace.

away

away

away

Write **away**.

_____

_____

Find each **away**. Color that space pink.
Then color the rest of the picture.

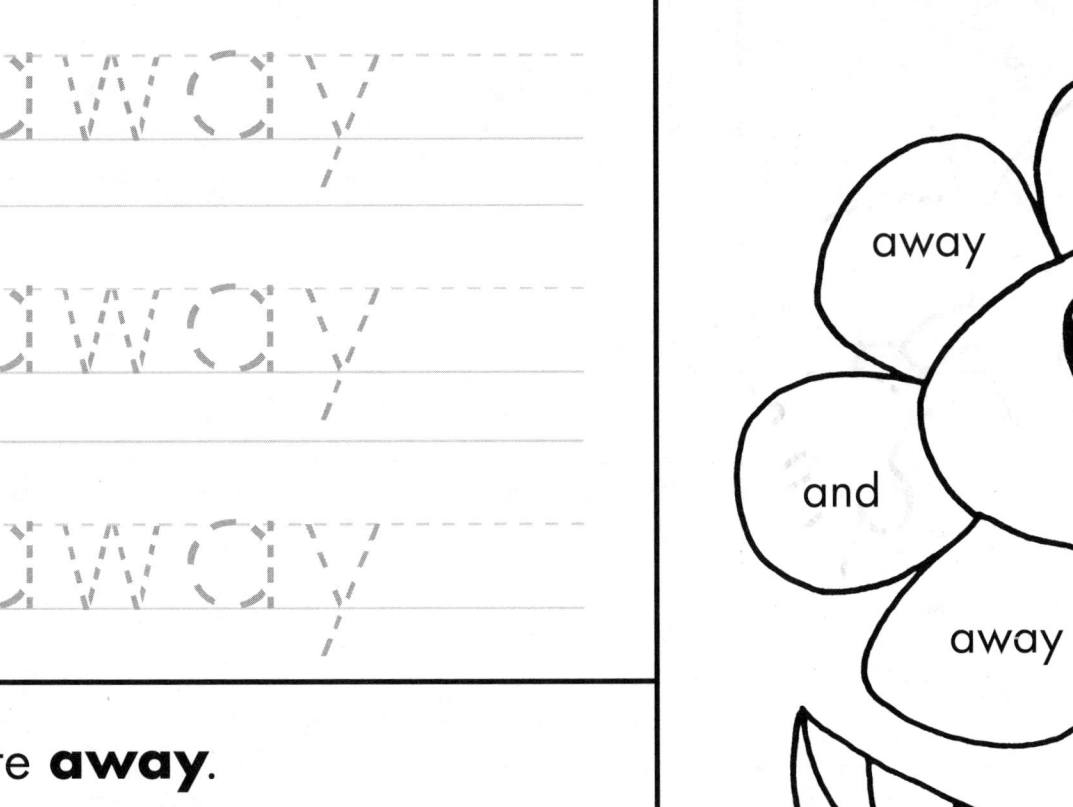

Name: _____

Trace.

be

be

be

Write **be**.

Find each **be**. Color that space yellow.
Then color the rest of the picture.

be

be

bun

by

be

bat

be

Trace.

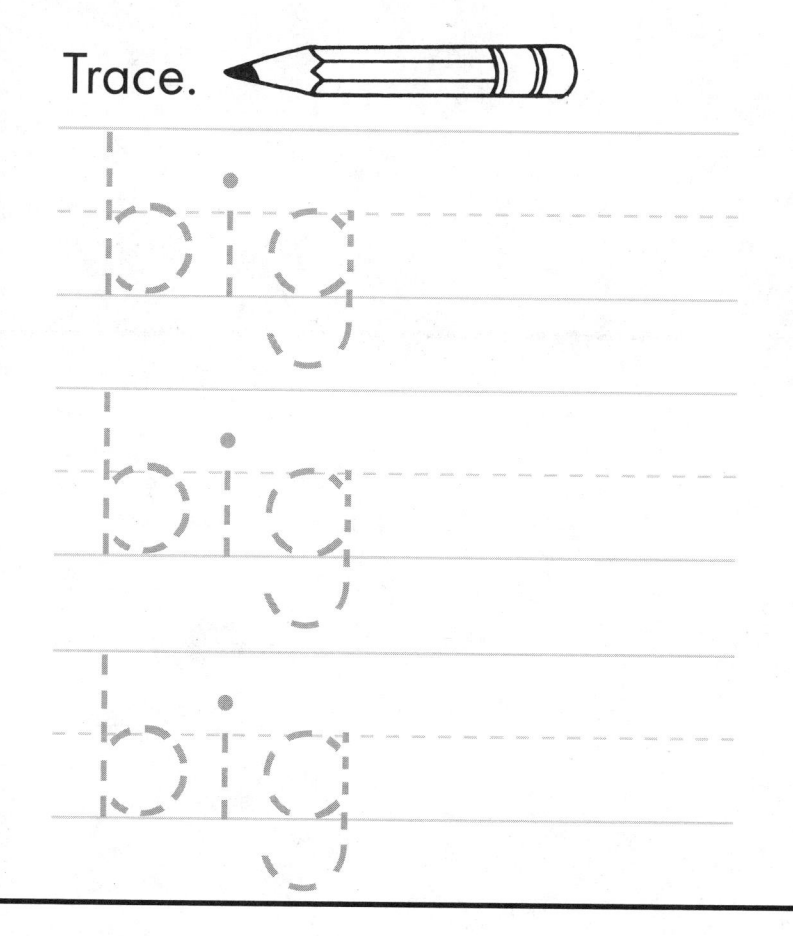

Write **big**.

Find each **big**. Color that owl brown. Then color the rest of the picture.

big   dig   big   bad

pig   big   dog   big

Name: _____

Trace.

blue

blue

blue

Write **blue**.

Find each **blue**. Color that bird blue.
Then color the rest of the picture.

Name: _____

Trace.

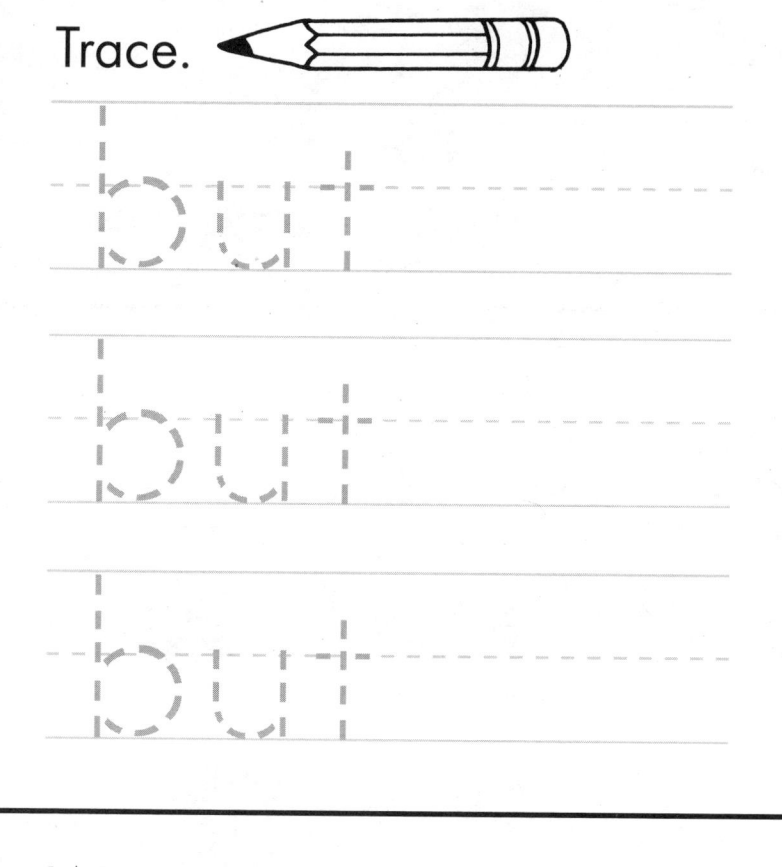

Write **but**.

_____

Find each **but**. Color that space purple.
Then color the rest of the picture.

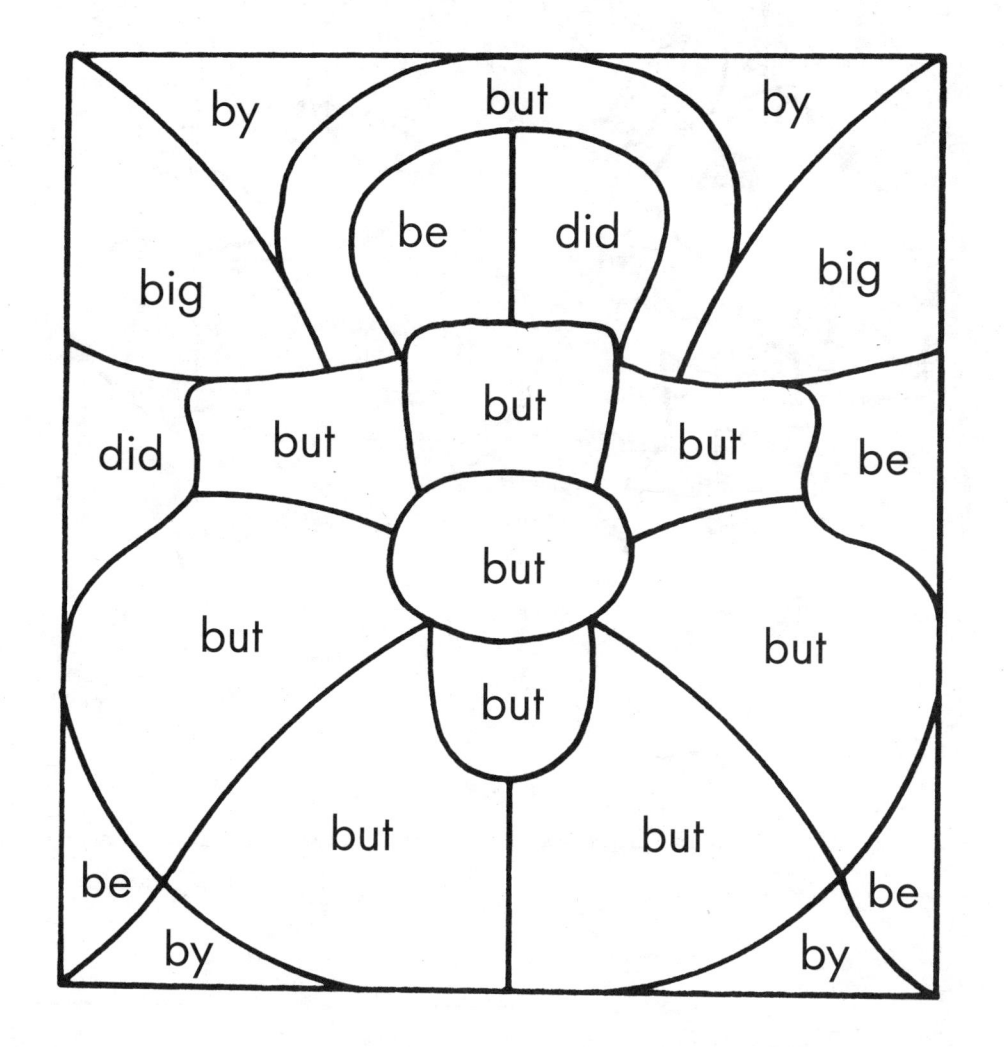

Name: _____

Trace.

by

by

by

Write **by**.

_____

_____

Find each **by**. Color that shape yellow.
Then color the rest of the picture.

by

but

boy

by

but

boy

by

be

be

by

Name: _____

Trace.

came

came

came

Write **came**.

_____

Find each **came**. Color that space orange. Then color the rest of the picture.

can

came

came

cone

come

came

came

can

Name: _____

Trace.

come

come

come

Write **come**.

Find each **come**. Color that mushroom red.
Then color the rest of the picture.

came   come   cone   come

come   can   come   came

Name: _____

Trace.

Find each **did**. Color that space green. Then color the rest of the picture.

Write **did**.

Name: _____

Trace.

do

do

do

Write **do**.

_____

Find each **do**. Color that space yellow.
Then color the rest of the picture.

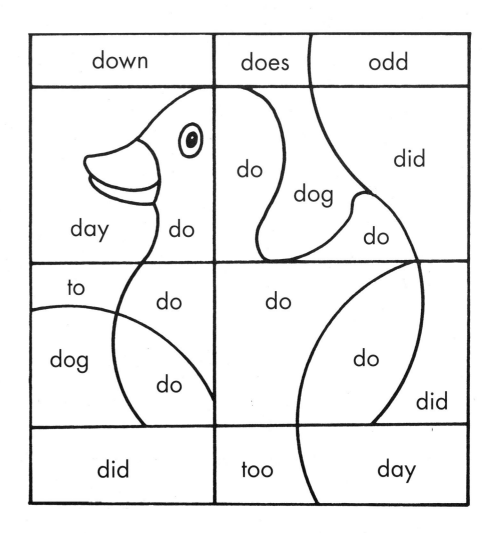

down	does	odd
		did
day	do	dog
to	do	do
dog	do	do did
did	too	day

Name: _____

Trace.

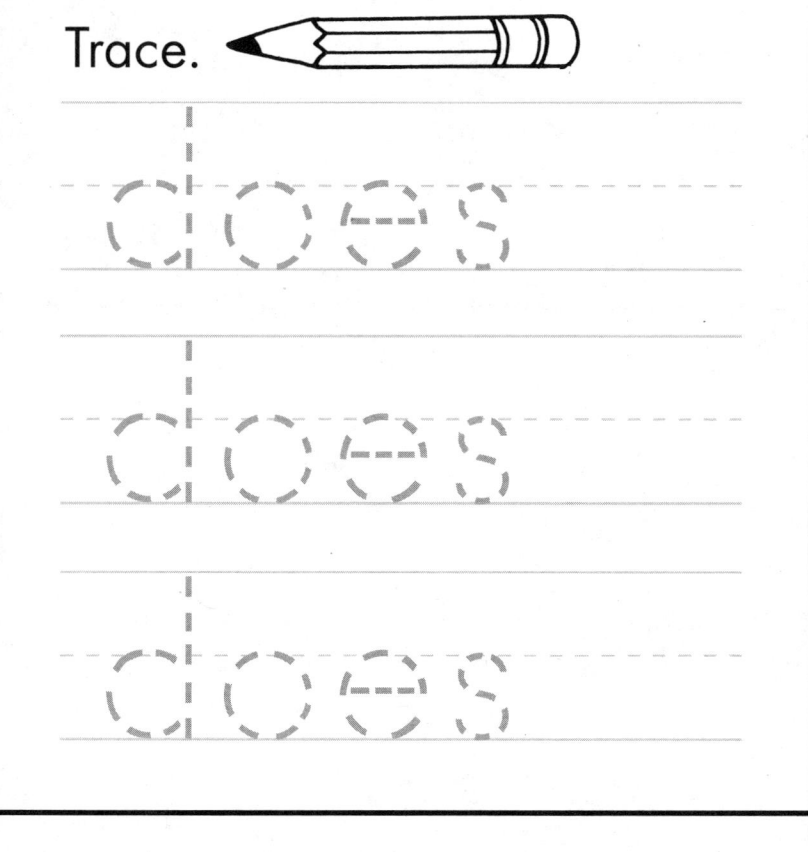

Write **does**.

_____

Find each **does**. Color that flower red. Then color the rest of the picture.

| do | does | does | den |

| does | toes | does | do |

Name: _____

Trace.

down

down

down

Write **down**.

Find each **down**. Color that space gray. Then color the rest of the picture.

Name: _____

Trace.

eat

eat

eat

Write **eat**.

_____

_____

Find each **eat**. Color that shape brown. Then color the rest of the picture.

eat

eat

at

set

at

eat

eat

cat

Name: _____

Trace.

find

find

find

Write **find**.

_____

_____

Find each **find**. Color that space orange. Then color the rest of the picture.

fin

find

find

fine

five

fine

find

find

fan

find

Trace.

Write **for**.

Find each **for**. Color that space red.
Then color the rest of the picture.

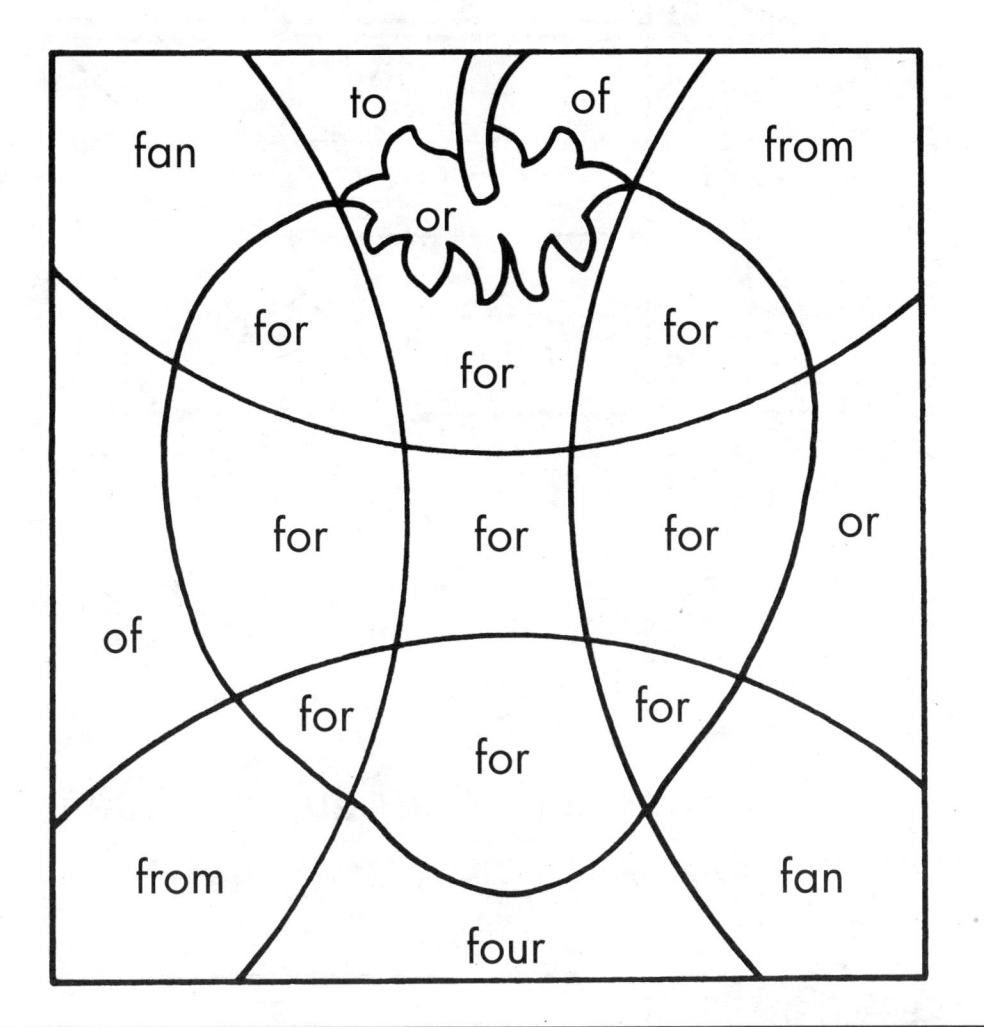

Name: _____

Trace.

found

found

found

Write **found**.

_____

Find each **found**. Color that gift purple. Then color the rest of the picture.

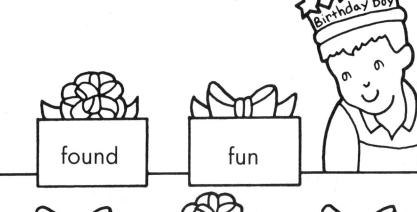

found	fun

find	found	four

found	fun	found

Name: _____

Trace.

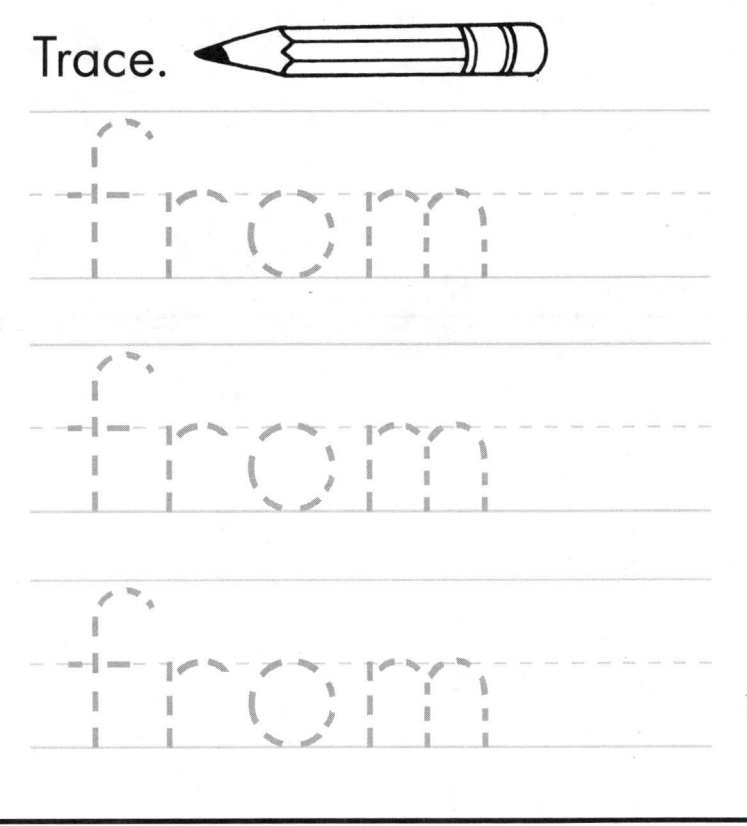

Write **from**.

Find each **from**. Color that penguin tan. Then color the rest of the picture.

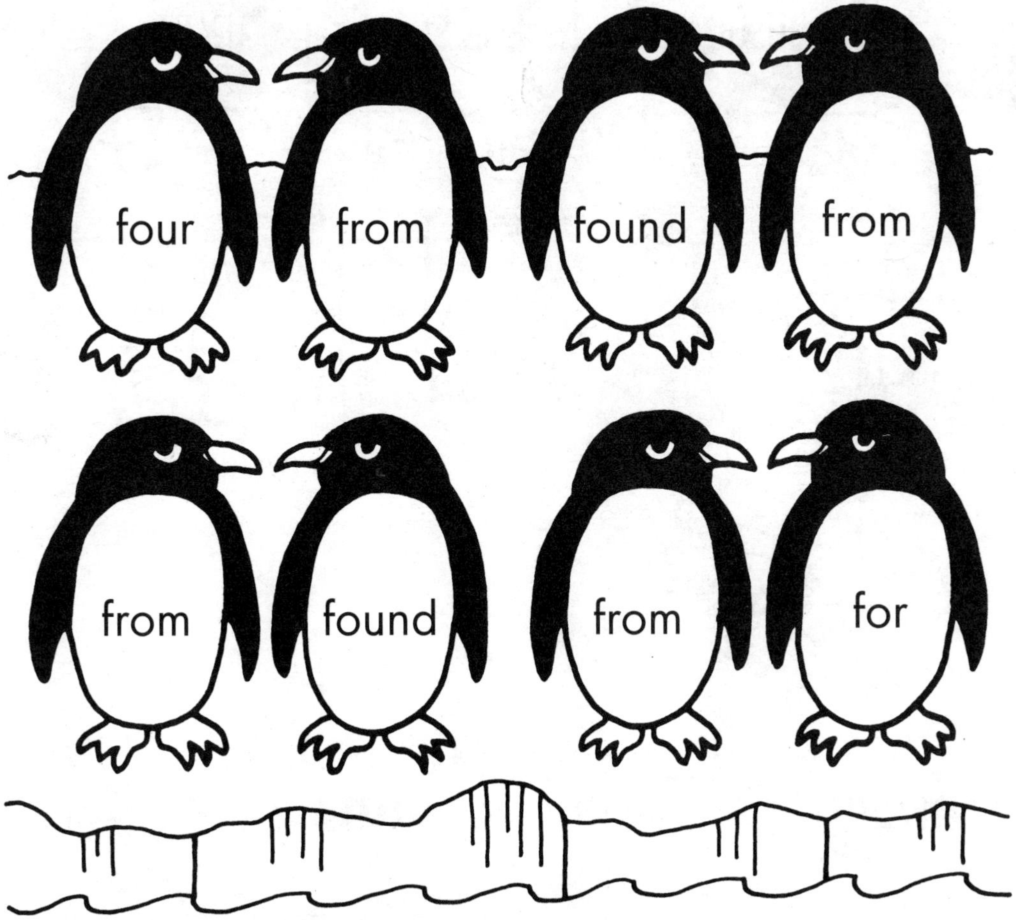

four   from   found   from

from   found   from   for

Name: _____

Trace.

Write **funny**.

_____

Find each **funny**. Color that lily pad green. Then color the rest of the picture.

Name: _____

Trace.

gave

gave

gave

Write **gave**.

_____

Find each **gave**. Color that mitten blue.
Then color the rest of the picture.

gave   have   gave   gate

gave   go   got   gave

Trace.

get

get

get

Write **get**.

get get get

Find each **get**. Color that ribbon blue. Then color the rest of the picture.

Name: _____

Trace.

go

go

go

Write **go**.

Find each **go**. Color that space red.
Then color the rest of the picture.

off

on

at

go

go

to

go

go

go

go

a

go

on

do

to

Trace.

goes

goes

goes

Write **goes**.

_____

goes

Find each **goes**. Color that space brown.
Then color the rest of the picture.

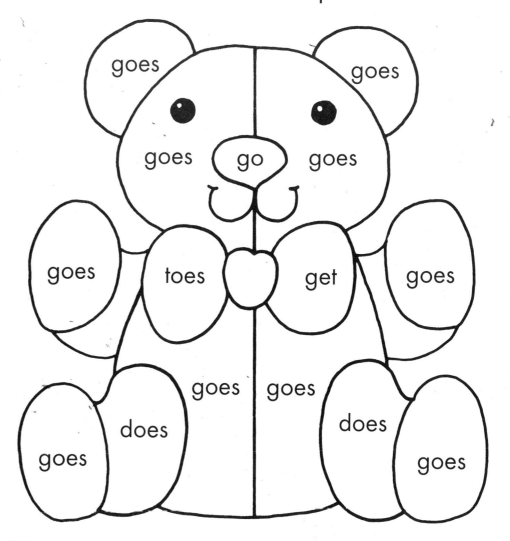

goes

goes

goes

go

goes

goes

toes

get

goes

goes

goes

goes

does

does

goes

goes

Name: _____

Trace.

good good good

Write **good**.

Find each **good**. Color that space pink.
Then color the rest of the picture.

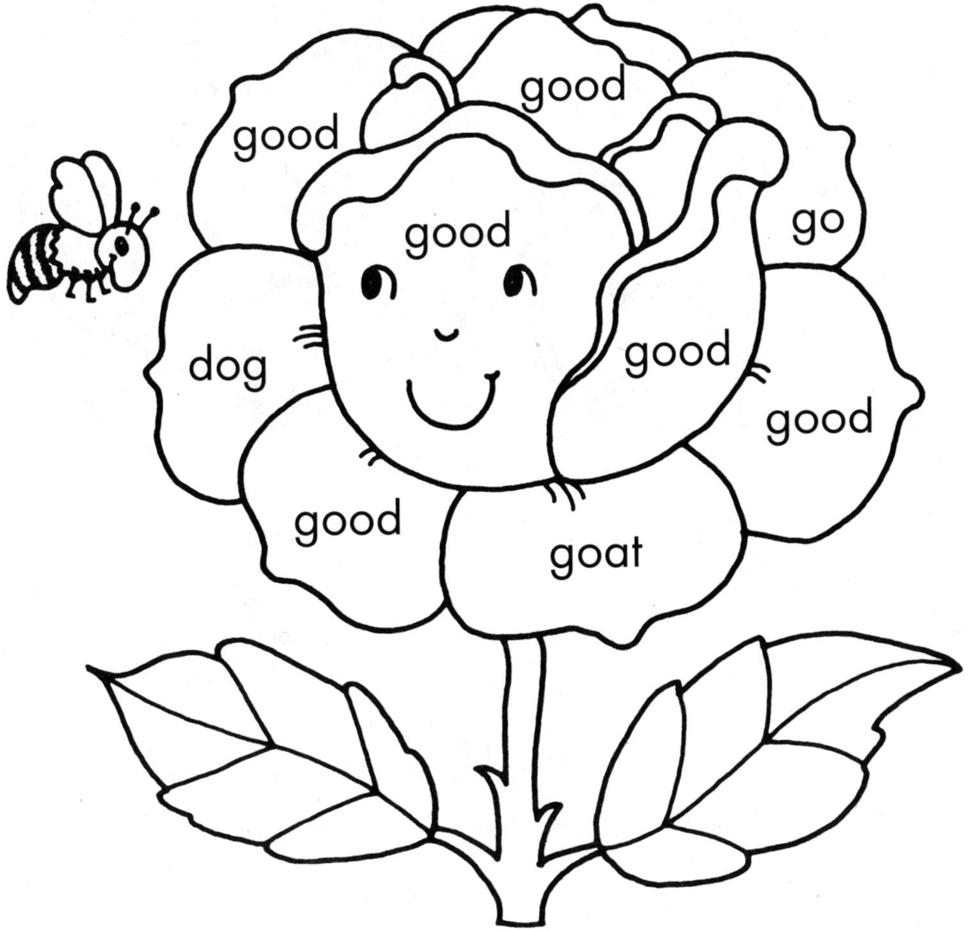

☆135☆   **Name:** _____

Sight Word: had

Trace.

had

had

had

Write **had**.

_____

_____

Find each **had**. Color that ball yellow.
Then color the rest of the picture.

dad

had

he

had

ham

add

had

had

Name: _____

Trace.

have

have

have

Write **have**.

Find each **have**. Color that space green.
Then color the rest of the picture.

have

have

had

have

wave

have

have

Name: _____

Trace.

he

he

he

Write **he**.

_____

Find each **he**. Color that space green.
Then color the rest of the picture.

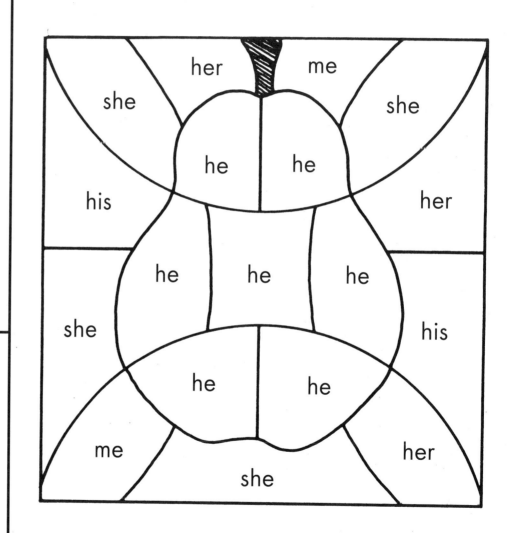

☆138☆ Name: _____

Trace.

help

help

help

Write **help**.

Find each **help**. Color that flag blue.
Then color the rest of the picture.

hop

help

hill

help

help

hop

hold

help

Name: _____

Trace.

her

her

her

Write **her**.

_____

Find each **her**. Color that space orange. Then color the rest of the picture.

her   he

hen

her   him

hit

her   her

Name: _____

Trace.

here

here

here

Write **here**.

_____

Find each **here**. Color that candle yellow. Then color the rest of the picture.

| her | here | help | here |

| here | he | here | hear |

Name: _____

Trace.

him

him

him

Write **him**.

Find each **him**. Color that apple red.
Then color the rest of the picture.

hen

his

him

him

he

her

him

him

☆142☆ Name: _____

Trace.

his

his

his

Write **his**.

Find each **his**. Color that space green.
Then color the rest of the picture.

is

it

hit

his

his

him

he

hen

his

him

his

he

Name: _____

Trace.

how

how

how

Write **how**.

_____

Find each **how**. Color that flower purple. Then color the rest of the picture.

Name: _____

Trace.

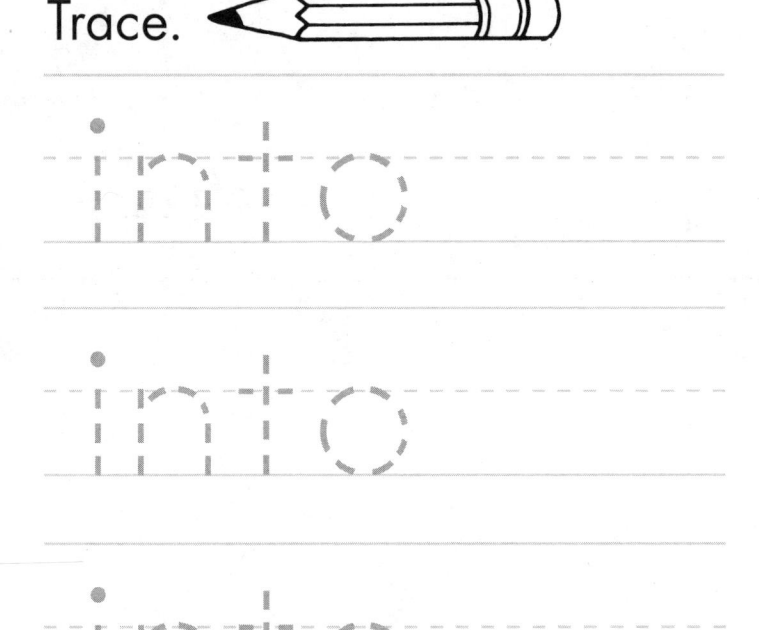

into

into

into

Write **into**.

_____

Find each **into**. Color that train car blue. Then color the rest of the picture.

| into | too | in |

| pin | into | fin |

| tin | into | into |

Name: _____

Trace.

is

is

is

Write **is**.

_____

Find each **is**. Color that space pink.
Then color the rest of the picture.

sit   his

it   in

is   is

is

is   is

is

his   is

sit   in

it

Name: _____

Trace.

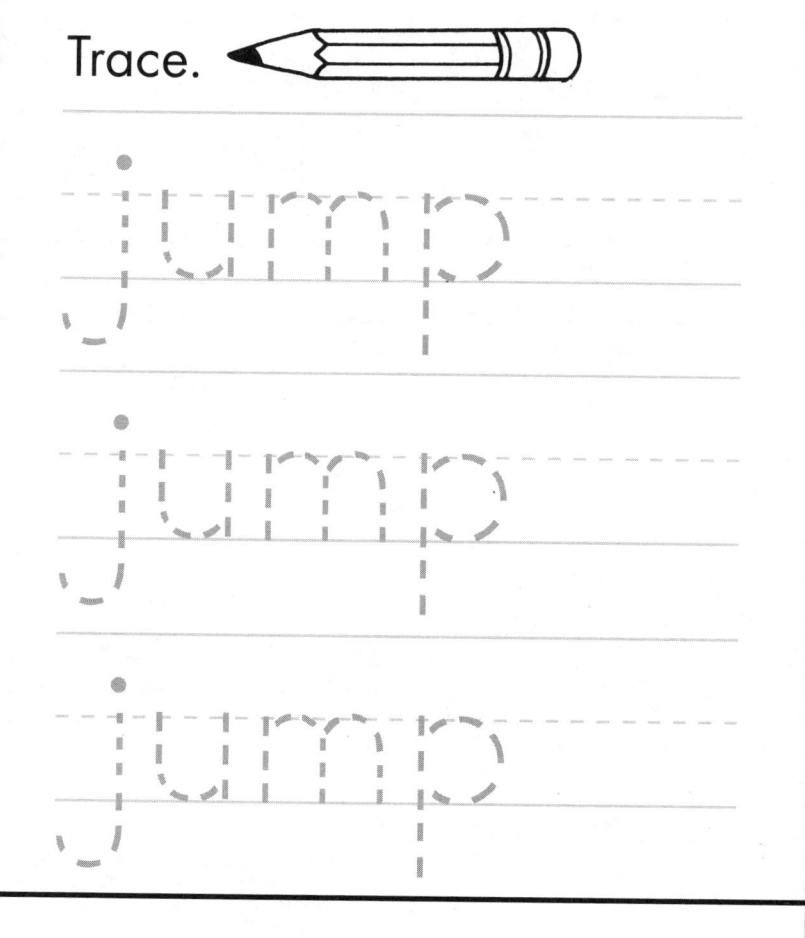

j u m p

j u m p

j u m p

Write **jump**.

_____

Find each **jump**. Color that space purple. Then color the rest of the picture.

jump

pump

just

jug

jug

jump

jam

bump

just

jump

jump

Name: _____

Trace.

j u s t

j u s t

j u s t

Write **just**.

_____

Find each **just**. Color that book brown.
Then color the rest of the picture.

jet

just

jump

just

jug

just

jump

just

Name: _____

Trace.

Write **like**.

Find each **like**. Color that pumpkin orange. Then color the rest of the picture.

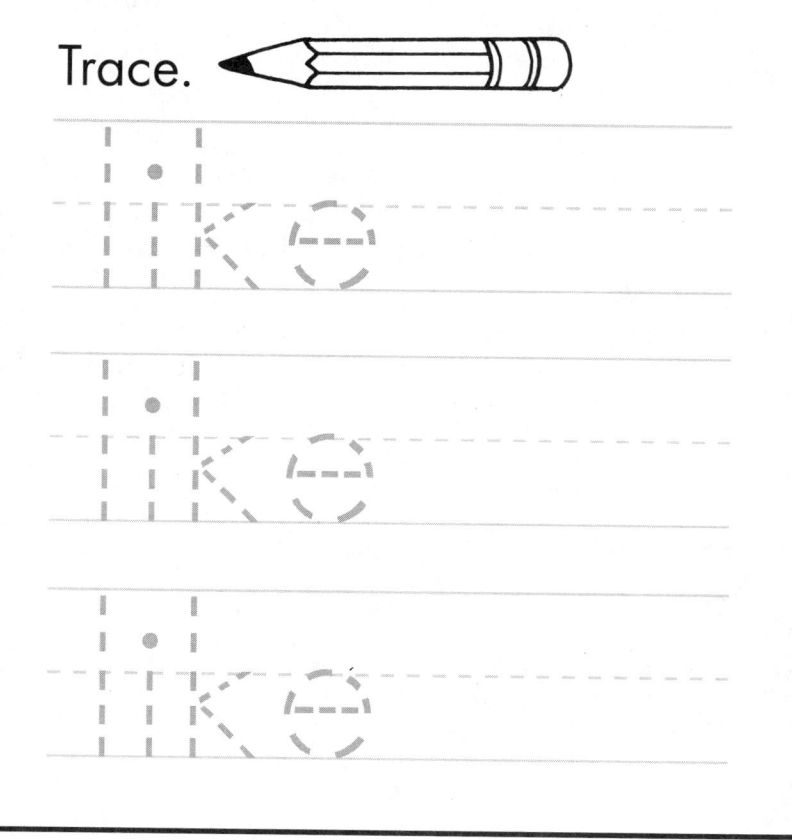

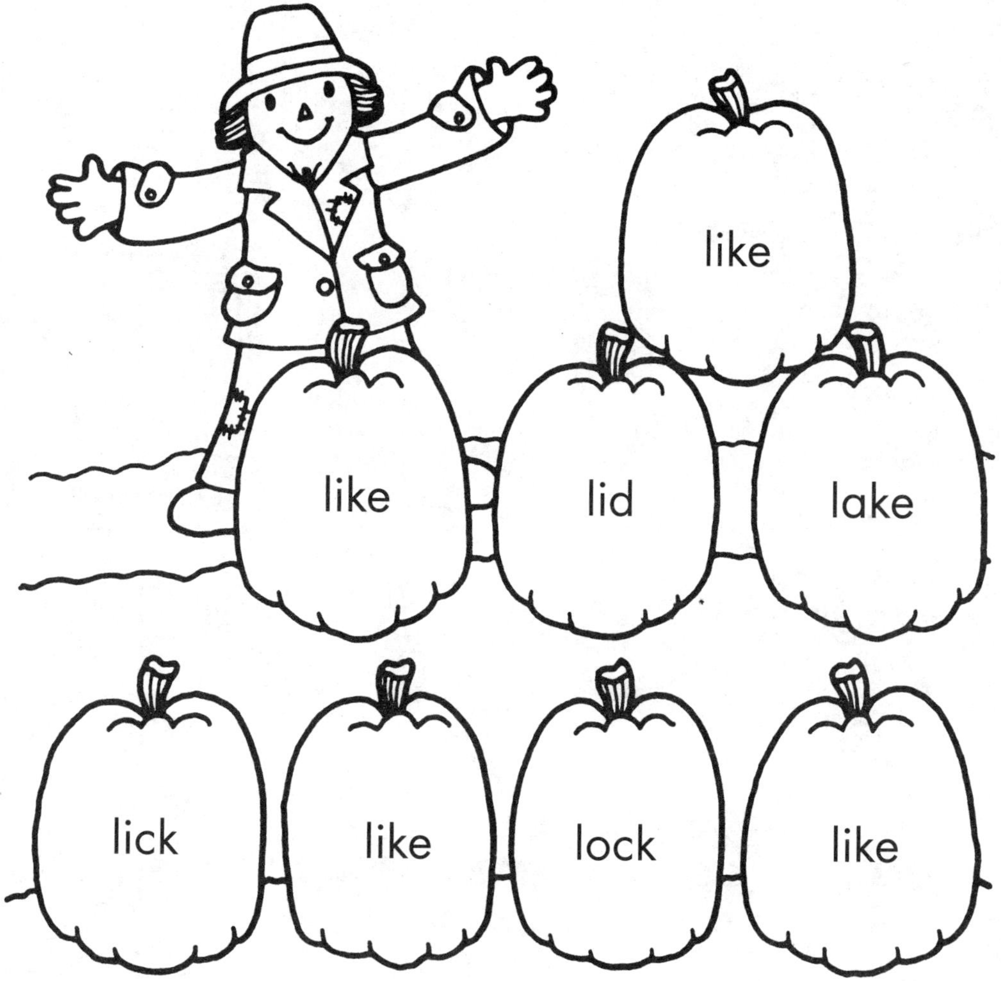

like

like   lid   lake

lick   like   lock   like

Name: _____

Trace.

little

little

little

Write **little**.

Find each **little**. Color that space black. Then color the rest of the picture.

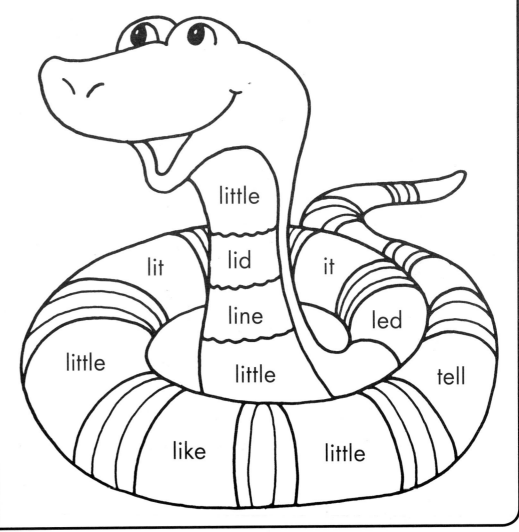

little

lit   lid   it

line   led

little   little   tell

like   little

Name: _____

Trace.

look

look

look

Write **look**.

_____

_____

Find each **look**. Color that acorn brown.
Then color the rest of the picture.

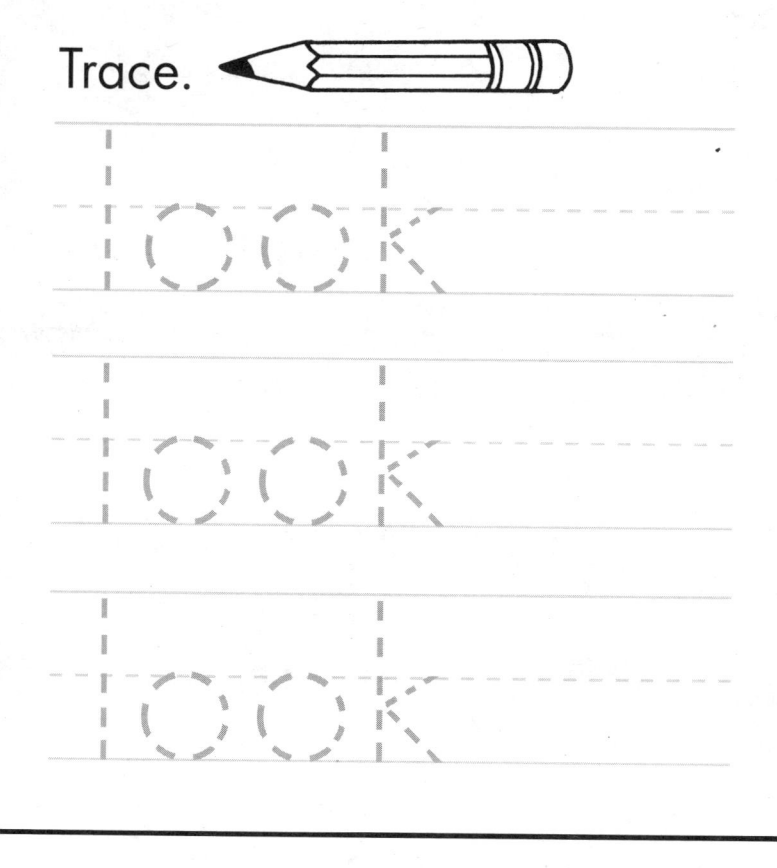

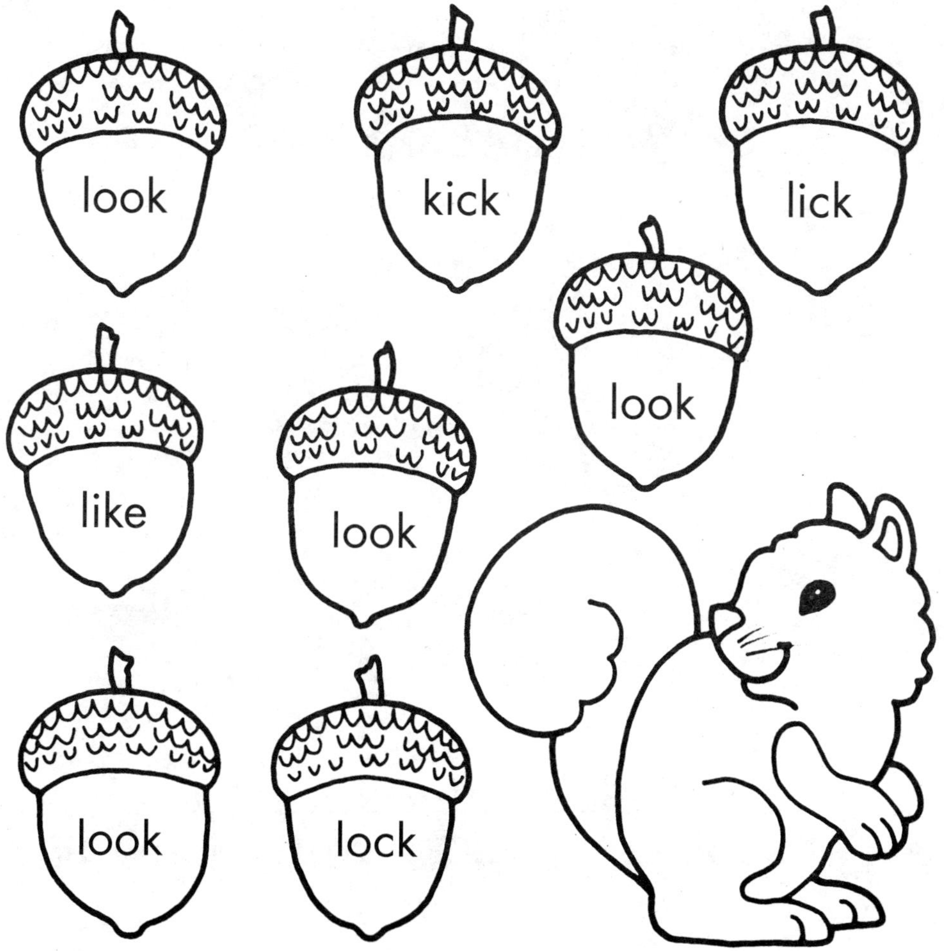

look   kick   lick

look

like   look

look   lock

Name: _____

Trace.

make

make

make

Write **make**.

_____

Find each **make**. Color that shell pink.
Then color the rest of the picture.

take

make

mate

made

make

make

make

mad

Name: _____

Trace.

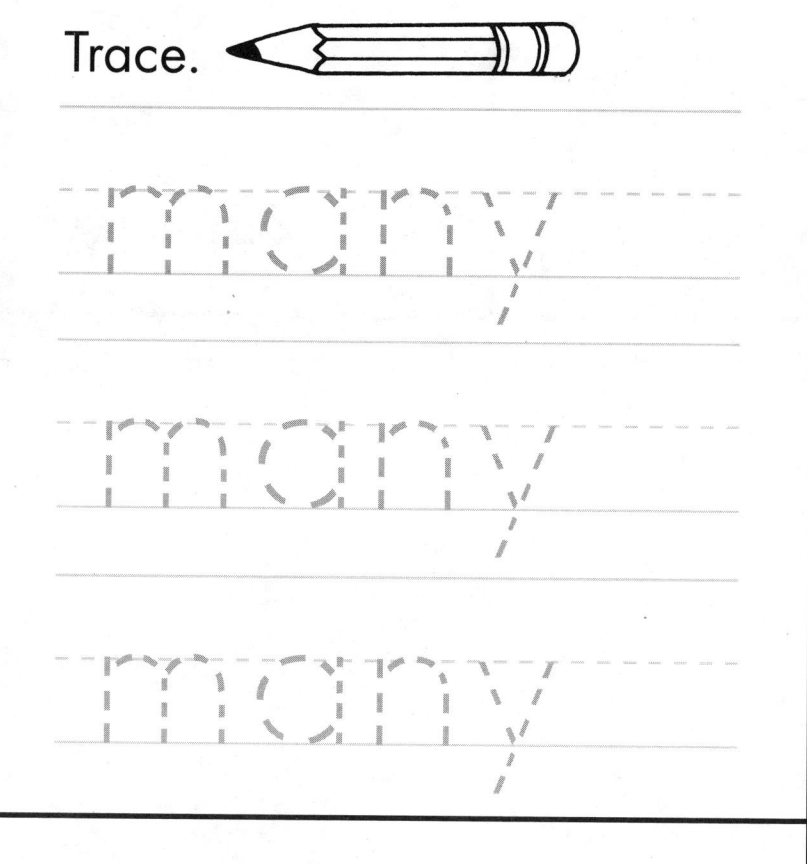

Write **many**.

Find each **many**. Color that cupcake yellow.
Then color the rest of the picture.

Name: _____

Trace.

my

my

my

Write **my**.

- - - - - - - - - - - - - -

Find each **my**. Color that space green.
Then color the rest of the picture.

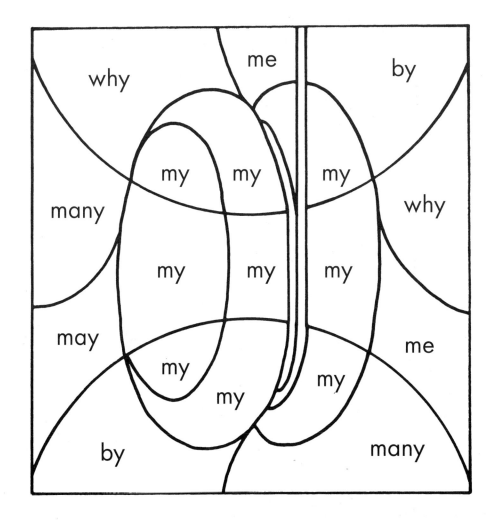

Name: _____

Trace.

new

new

new

Write **new**.

Find each **new**. Color that space red.
Then color the rest of the picture.

men

now

new

net

new

new

new

no

Happy
Birthday

new

Name: _____

Trace.

no

no

no

Write **no**.

Find each **no**. Color that bowling pin purple. Then color the rest of the picture.

no

now

no

not

on

no

an

no

Name: _____

Trace.

Write **not**.

_____

Find each **not**. Color that snowflake blue. Then color the rest of the picture.

☆157☆ Name: _____

Sight Word: now

Trace.

now

now

now

Write **now**.

Find each **now**. Color that space orange.
Then color the rest of the picture.

now

now   won

row

no

on

not

now

now

Now I Know My Word Families & Sight Words © 2012 Scholastic Teaching Resources • page 173

Name: _____

Trace.

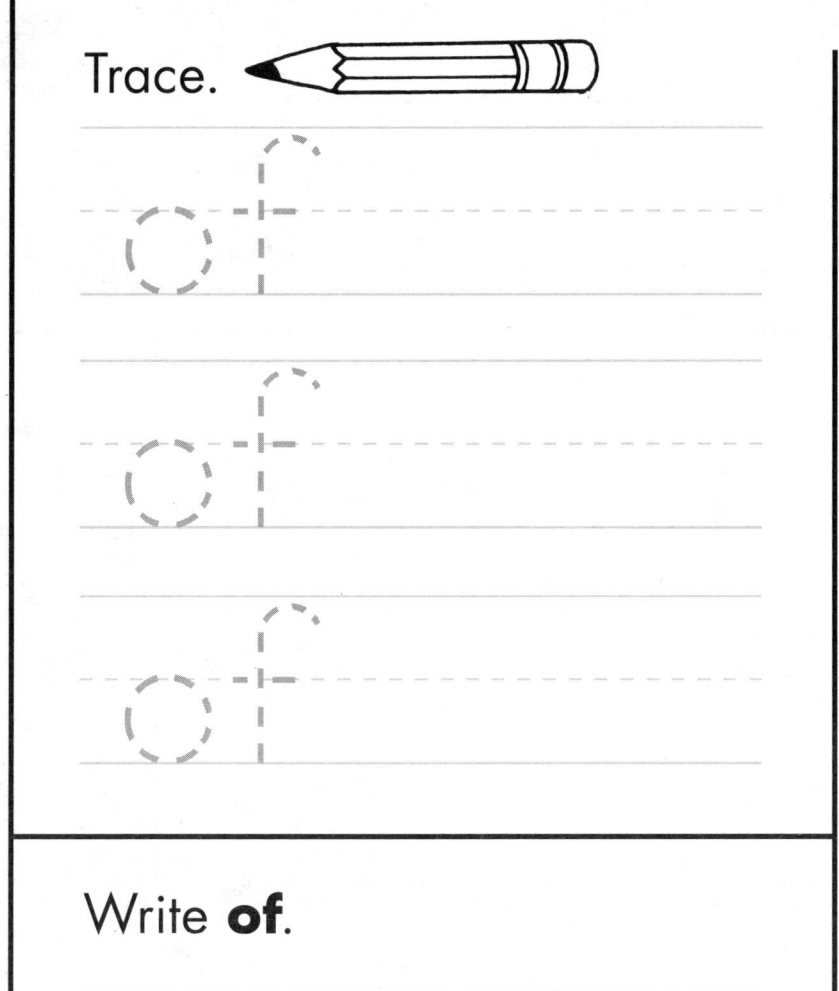

Write **of**.

Find each **of**. Color that space brown. Then color the rest of the picture.

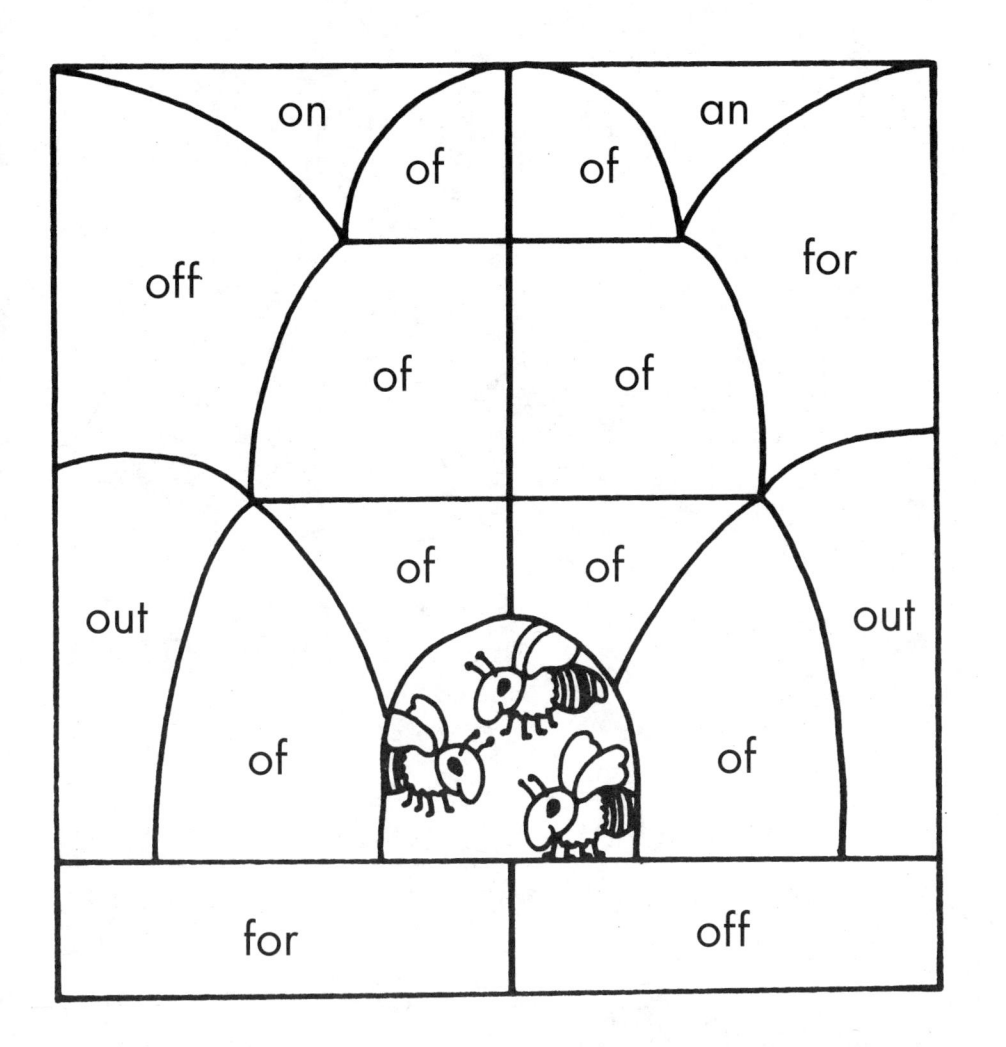

Trace.

o f f

o f f

o f f

Write **off**.

_____

Find each **off**. Color that heart red.
Then color the rest of the picture.

off

of

for

off

fun

off

off

on

Name: _____

Trace.

on

on

on

Write **on**.

_____

Find each **on**. Color that toy blue.
Then color the rest of the picture.

now   on   one   on

on   on   an   no

Name: _____

Trace.

our

our

our

Write **our**.

Find each **our**. Color that space black. Then color the rest of the picture.

Name: _____

Trace.

out

out

out

Write **out**.

Find each **out**. Color that space brown.
Then color the rest of the picture.

our

out

on

of

out

out

own

our

out

out

Name: _____

Trace.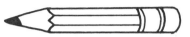

over

over

over

Write **over**.

_____

Find each **over**. Color that wing gray. Then color the rest of the picture.

Name: _____

Trace.

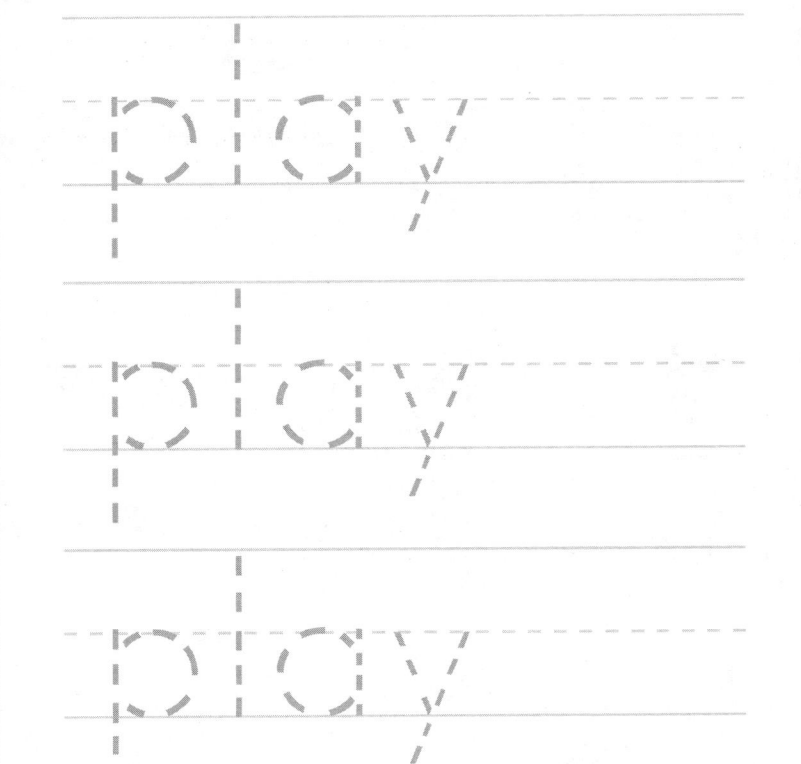

Write **play**.

_____

Find each **play**. Color that space pink.
Then color the rest of the picture.

Name: _____

Trace.

please

please

please

Write **please**.

Find each **please**. Color that space purple. Then color the rest of the picture.

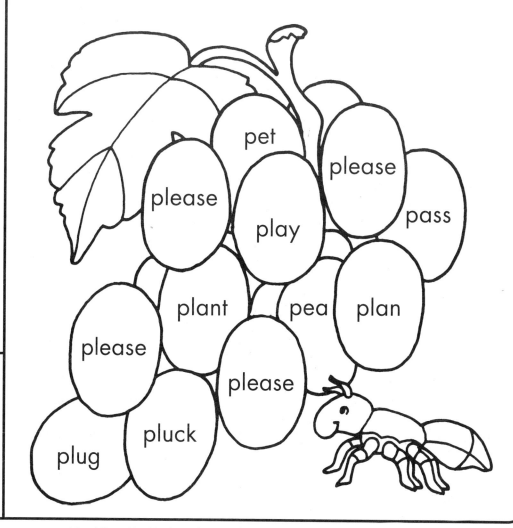

pet

please

please

play

pass

plant

pea

plan

please

please

plug

pluck

Name: _____

Trace.

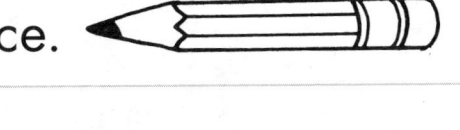

pretty

pretty

pretty

Write **pretty**.

_____

Find each **pretty**. Color that space yellow. Then color the rest of the picture.

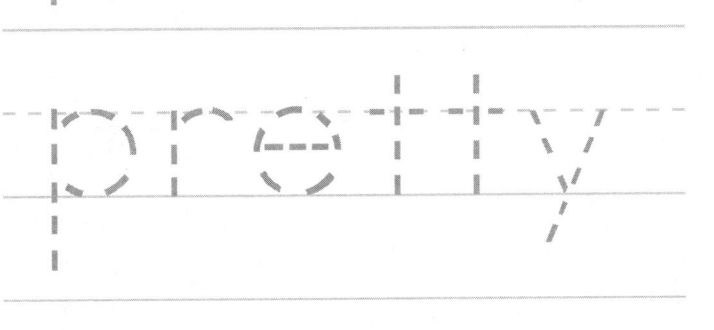

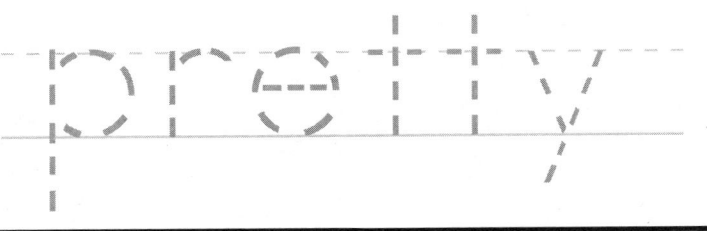

pet

pretty   pretty

pray   pretty   press   pet

pet   print   pretty   put

Trace.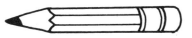

put

put

put

Write **put**.

_____

Find each **put**. Color that space green.
Then color the rest of the picture.

Trace. ✏️

read

read

read

Write **read**.

_____

Find each **read**. Color that space orange.
Then color the rest of the picture.

red
read
deer
read
read
dad
rear
read

Trace.

red
red
red

Write **red**.

Find each **red**. Color that space red. Then color the rest of the picture.

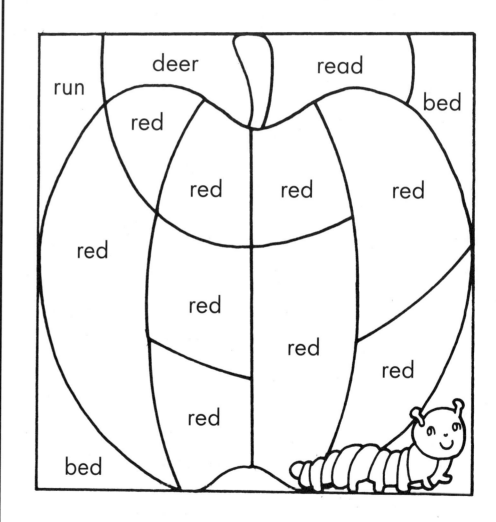

Trace.

ride

ride

ride

Write **ride**.

_____

_____

Find each **ride**. Color that space blue. Then color the rest of the picture.

read

ride

ride

it

in

rid

red

ride

side

ride

rip

run

Name: _____

Trace.

right

right

right

Write **right**.

_____

_____

Find each **right**. Color that bone gray.
Then color the rest of the picture.

right

night

tight

ride

right

right

right

ripe

Name: _____

Trace.

run

run

run

Find each **run**. Color that space orange.
Then color the rest of the picture.

run   nut   run   red

can   run   ran   run

Write **run**.

_____

Name: _____

Trace.

said

said

said

Write **said**.

Find each **said**. Color that space brown. Then color the rest of the picture.

said

say

said

see

so

said

raid

said

 ☆174☆

Name: _____

Trace.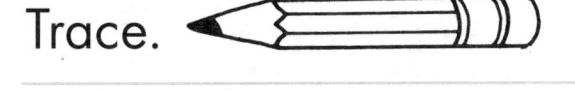

saw

saw

saw

Write **saw**.

Find each **saw**. Color that butterfly purple. Then color the rest of the picture.

say

saw

so

said

saw

saw

was

saw

Name: _____

Trace.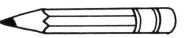

say

say

say

Write **say**.

_____

Find each **say**. Color that space gray.
Then color the rest of the picture.

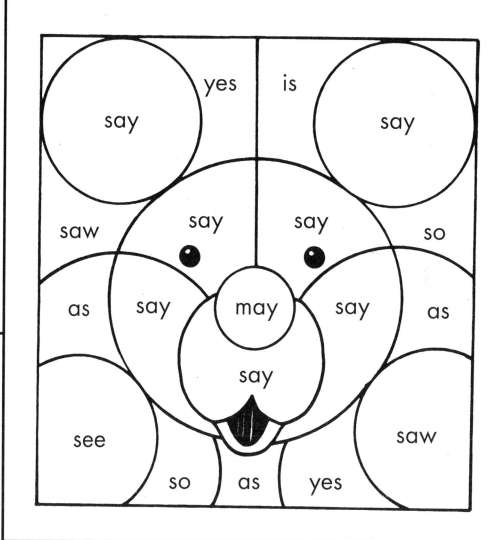

Name: _____

Trace.

see

see

see

Write **see**.

_____

Find each **see**. Color that bee yellow.
Then color the rest of the picture.

saw see so see

she seen

see see

☆177☆ Name: _____

Trace.

she

she

she

Write **she**.

_____

Find each **she**. Color that space green.
Then color the rest of the picture.

she

her   shoe

the

she

he   see

she   his   she

Trace.

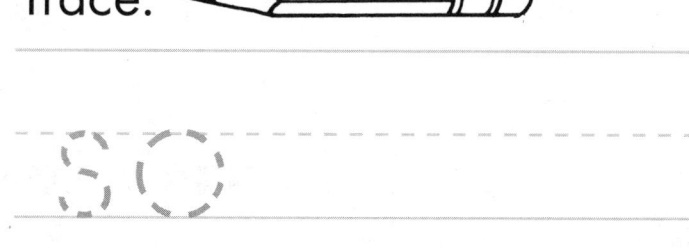

Write **so**.

Find each **so**. Color that space yellow. Then color the rest of the picture.

Name: _____

Trace.

some

some

some

Write **some**.

_____

Find each **some**. Color that balloon red. Then color the rest of the picture.

☆180☆ **Name:** _____

Trace.

soon

soon

soon

Write **soon**.

_____

Find each **soon**. Color that tree green.
Then color the rest of the picture.

soon   so   son   soon

soon   some   so   soon

Trace.

that

that

that

Write **that**.

Find each **that**. Color that ribbon blue.
Then color the rest of the picture.

that   hat   bat

then   that

that   that   the

Trace.

the

the

the

Write **the**.

Find each **the**. Color that space gray. Then color the rest of the picture.

the

then

ten

the

the

too

that

the

Name: _____

Trace.

their

their

their

Write **their**.

_____

_____

_____

Find each **their**. Color that space purple.
Then color the rest of the picture.

Name: _____

Trace.

Find each **them**. Color that space green. Then color the rest of the picture.

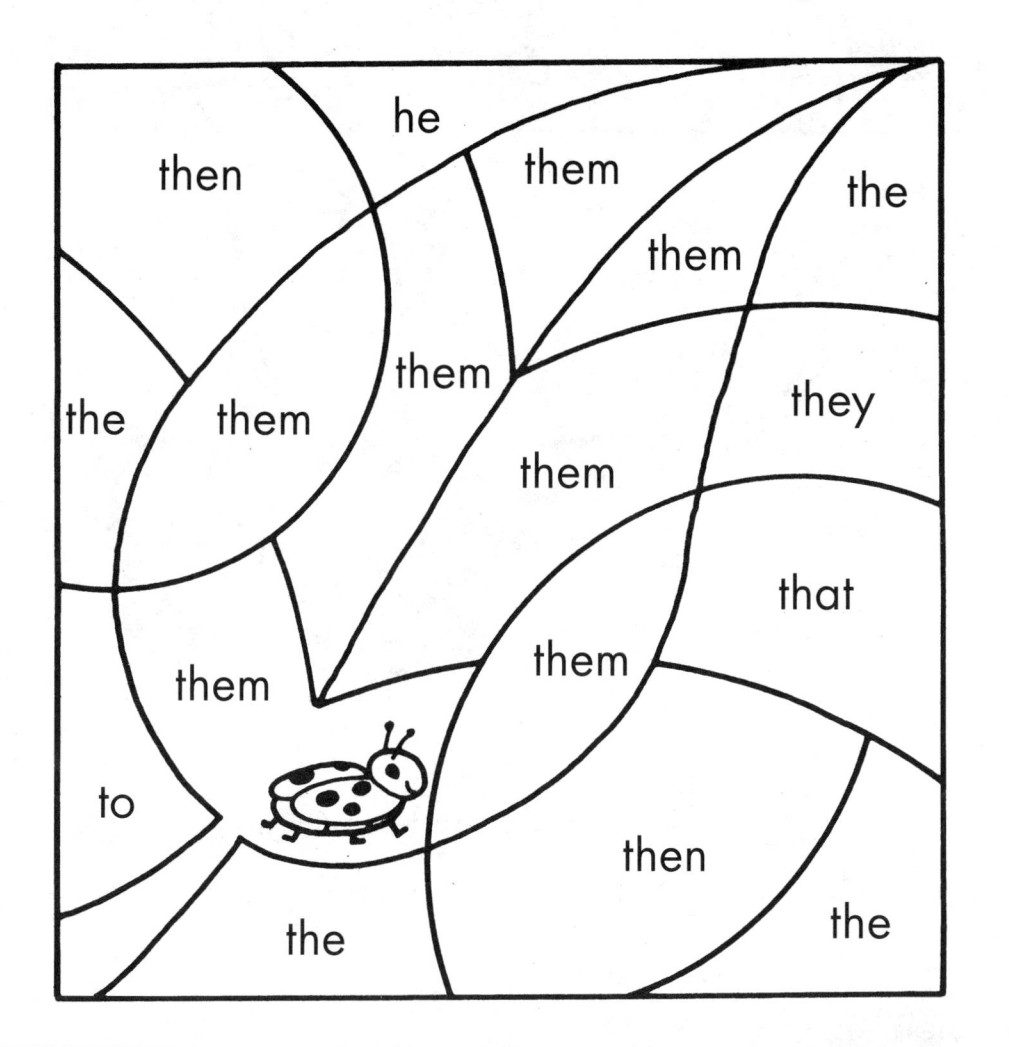

Write **them**.

Name: _____

Trace.

then

then

then

Write **then**.

_____

_____

Find each **then**. Color that strawberry red. Then color the rest of the picture.

them

then

then

hen

then

the

they

then

then

Name: _____

Trace. ✏️

there

there

there

Write **there**.

_____

Find each **there**. Color that space brown. Then color the rest of the picture.

there

them

there

the   there

then

there   their

Name: _____

Trace.

they

they

they

Write **they**.

Find each **they**. Color that space orange. Then color the rest of the picture.

they

the

they

they

them

he

hay

then

they

Name: _____

Trace.

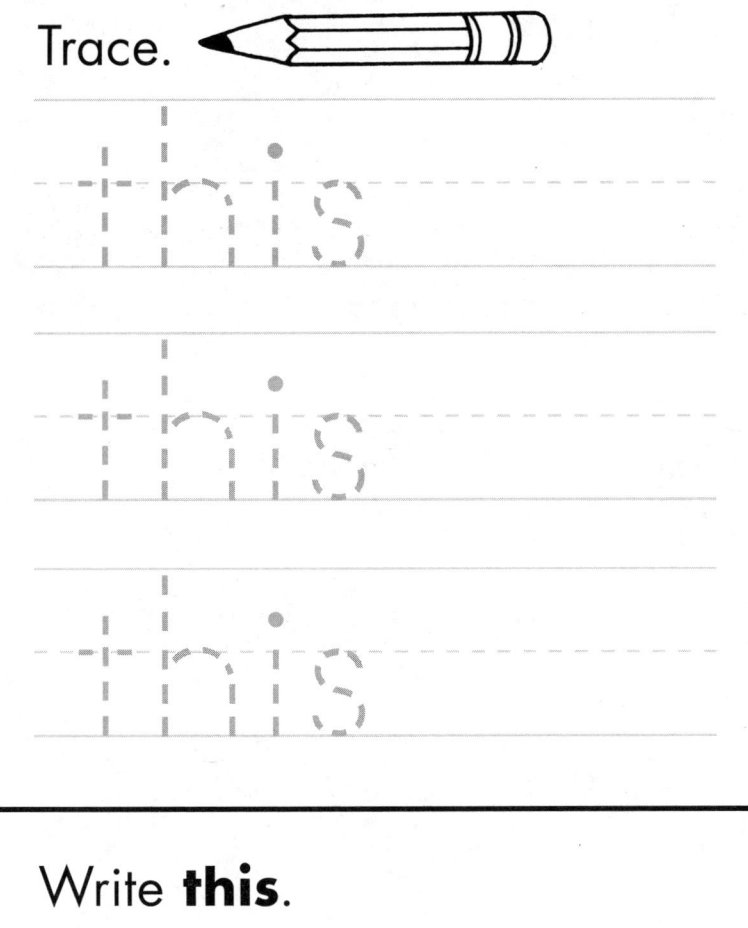

Write **this**.

Find each **this**. Color that rocket blue. Then color the rest of the picture.

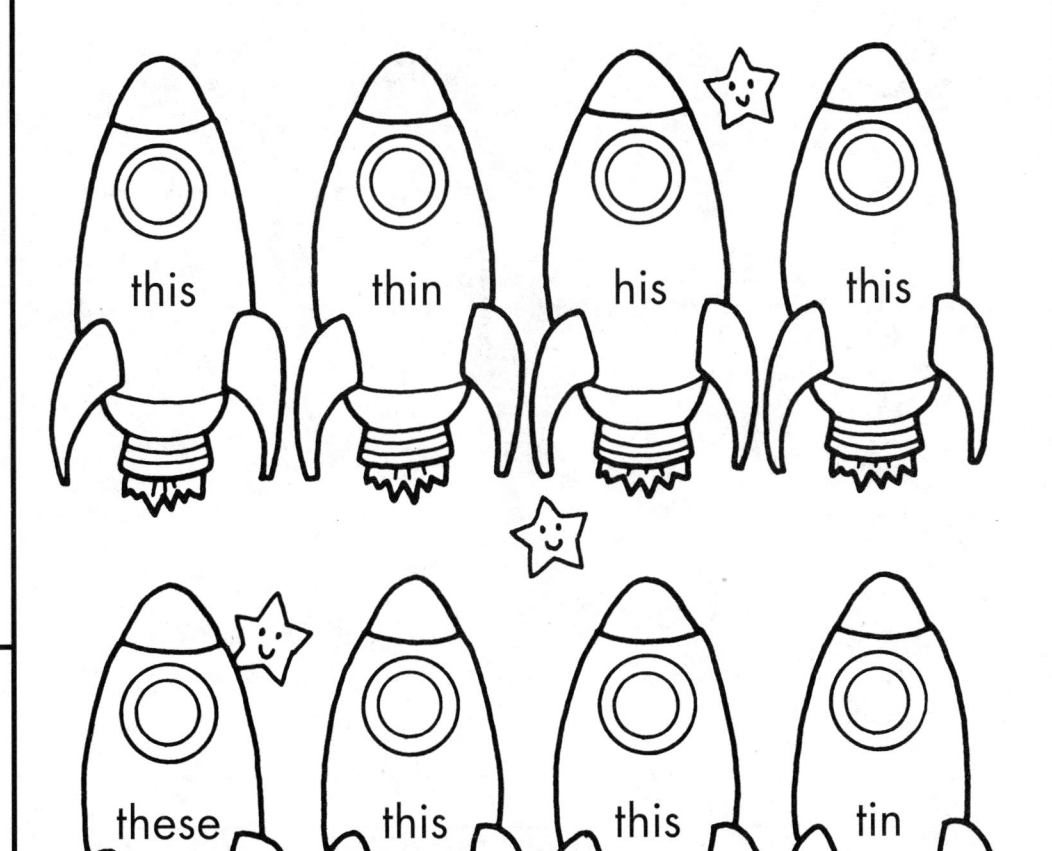

this   thin   his   this

these   this   this   tin

Name: _____

Trace.

too

too

too

Write **too**.

_____

Find each **too**. Color that space red.
Then color the rest of the picture.

ton

too

toe

too

out

to

too

too

Name: _____

Trace.

under

under

under

Write **under**.

_____

_____

Find each **under**. Color that cup pink.
Then color the rest of the picture.

fun

under

under

drum

mud

under

under

run

Name: _____

Trace.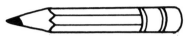

Us

Us

Us

Write **us**.

_____

Find each **us**. Color that space yellow.
Then color the rest of the picture.

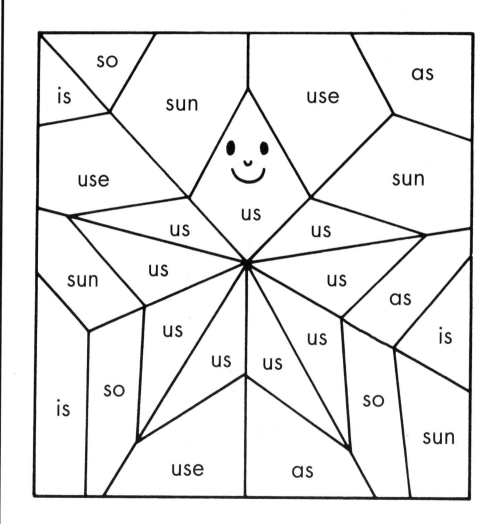

Name: _____

Trace.

very

very

very

Write **very**.

Find each **very**. Color that space black.
Then color the rest of the picture.

very   way

vase   very   very   yes

very

wave

very

Trace.

want

want

want

Write **want**.

_____

Find each **want**. Color that jellybean red. Then color the rest of the picture.

want	what	want	went

was	want	want	west

Name: _____

Trace.

was

was

was

Write **was**.

_____

_____

Find each **was**. Color that cracker orange. Then color the rest of the picture.

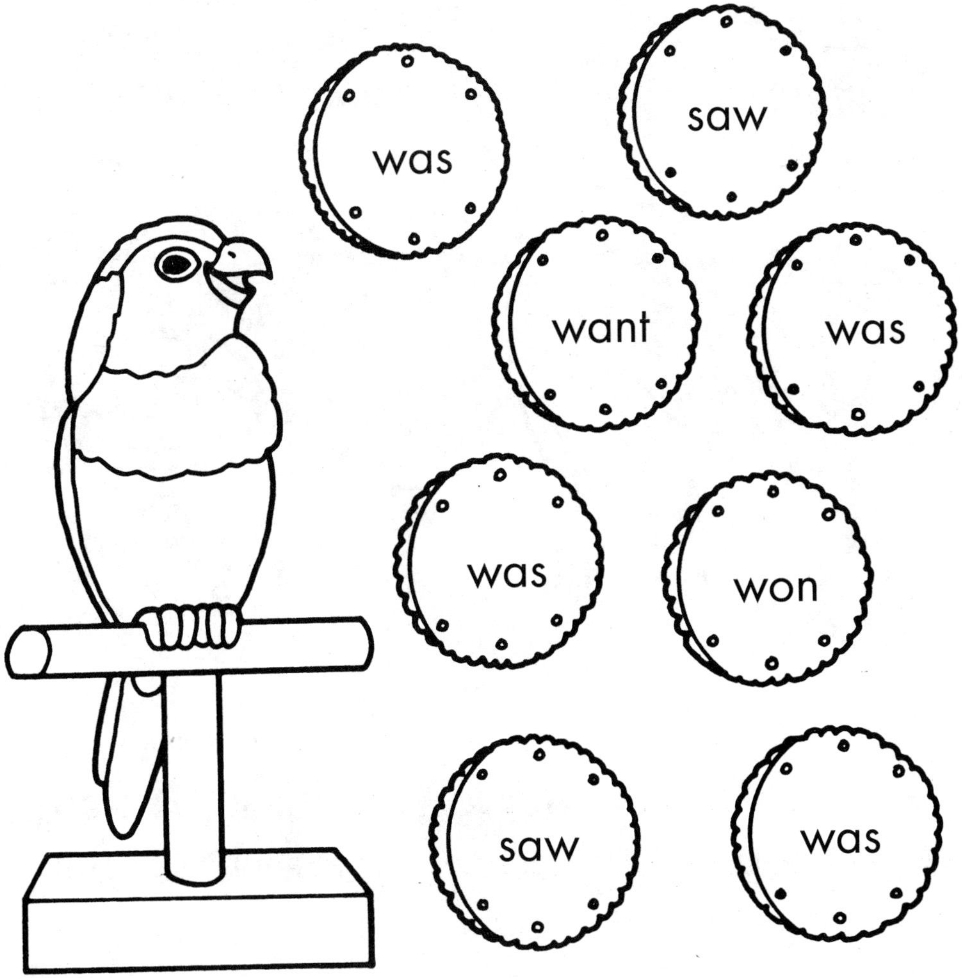

was

saw

want

was

was

won

saw

was

Name: _____

Trace.

well

well

well

Write **well**.

_____

Find each **well**. Color that bear brown. Then color the rest of the picture.

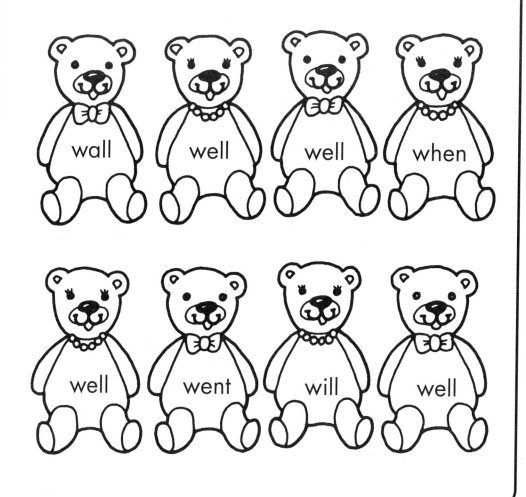

wall   well   well   when

well   went   will   well

Trace.

Write **went**.

_____

Find each **went**. Color that pencil yellow. Then color the rest of the picture.

went

new

want

went

went

when

win

went

Name: _____

Trace.

were

were

were

Write **were**.

_____

Find each **were**. Color that space blue. Then color the rest of the picture.

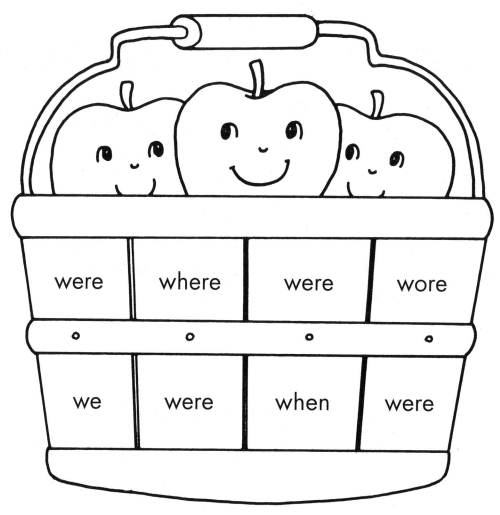

| were | where | were | wore |
| we | were | when | were |

Trace.

what

what

what

Write **what**.

_____

Find each **what**. Color that ball green.
Then color the rest of the picture.

what

hat

went

what

what

when

what

want

Name: _____

Trace.

when

when

when

Write **when**.

_____

Find each **when**. Color that pie brown.
Then color the rest of the picture.

Name: _____

Trace.

where

where

where

Write **where**.

_____

Find each **where**. Color that space yellow. Then color the rest of the picture.

Name: _____

Sight Word: who

Trace.

who

who

who

Write **who**.

_____

Find each **who**. Color that space orange.
Then color the rest of the picture.

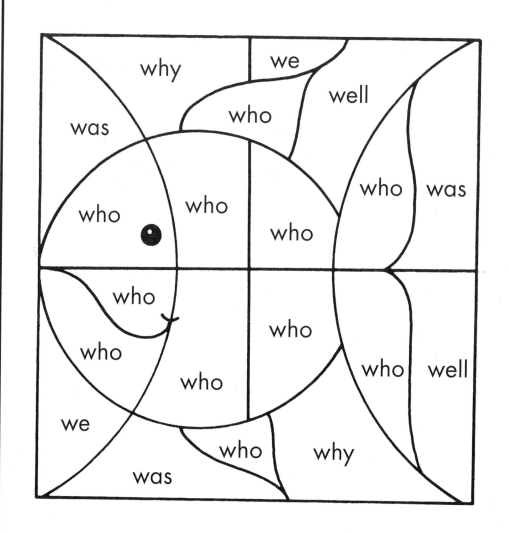

☆ 202 ☆

Name: _____

Trace.

~~will~~

~~will~~

~~will~~

Write **will**.

- - - - - - - - - - - - - -

Find each **will**. Color that float yellow.
Then color the rest of the picture.

with

will

win

will

hill

will

mill

will

Name: _____

Trace.

with

with

with

Write **with**.

_____

Find each **with**. Color that bag red.
Then color the rest of the picture.

with

will

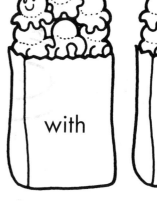

with

wind

win

with

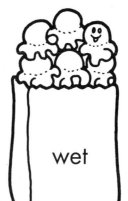

wet

with

☆204☆ Name: _____

Trace.

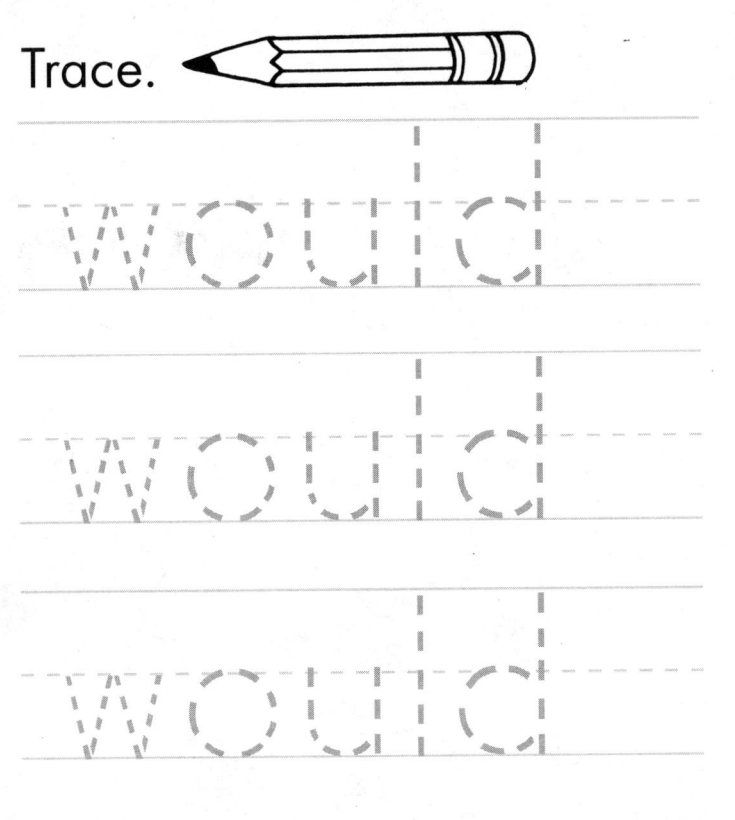

Write **would**.

_____

Find each **would**. Color that sail purple. Then color the rest of the picture.

cold would could

would down

would worm would

Trace.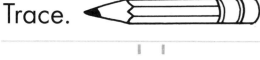

yellow

yellow

yellow

Write **yellow**.

_____

_____

Find each **yellow**. Color that flower yellow. Then color the rest of the picture.

☆206☆ Name: _____

Trace.

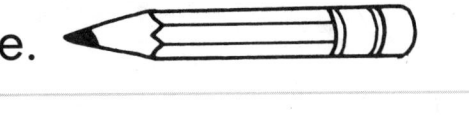

Write **yes**.

Find each **yes**. Color that space orange. Then color the rest of the picture.

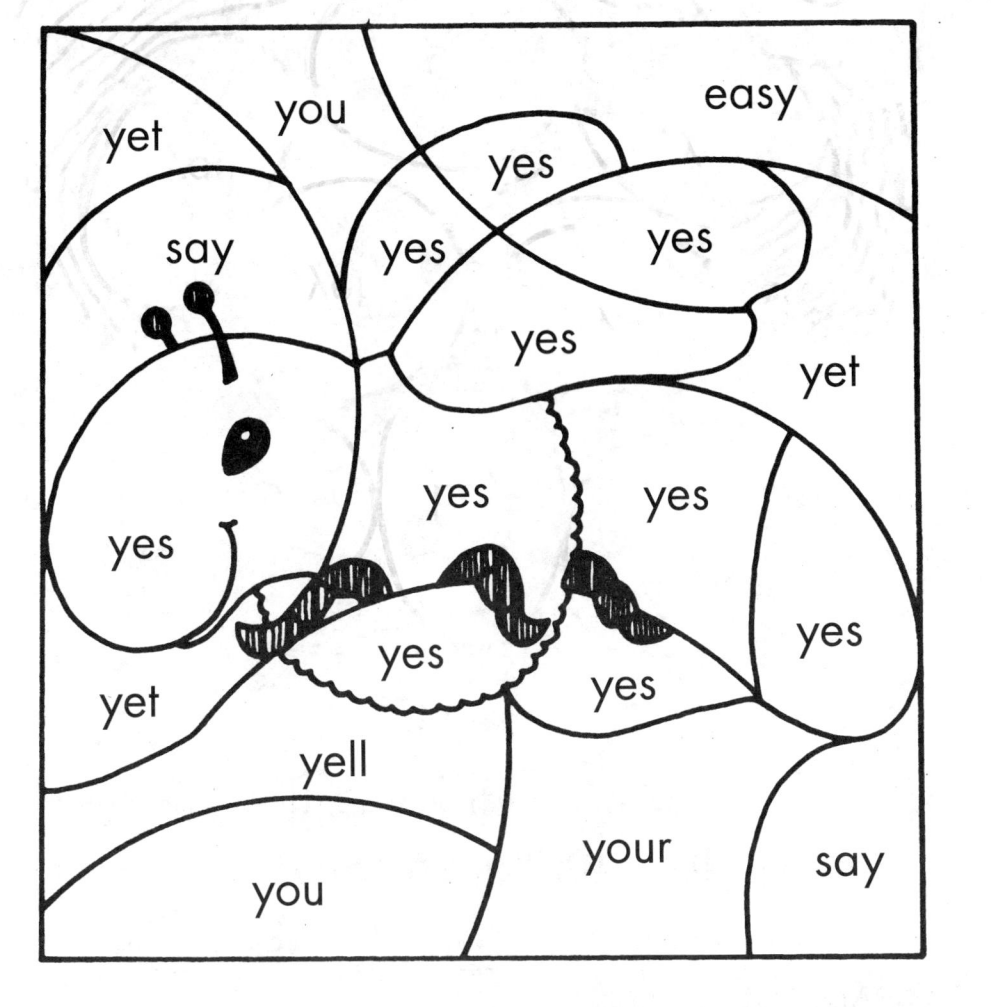

Trace.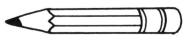

y o u

y o u

y o u

Write **you**.

_____

Find each **you**. Color that egg brown.
Then color the rest of the picture.

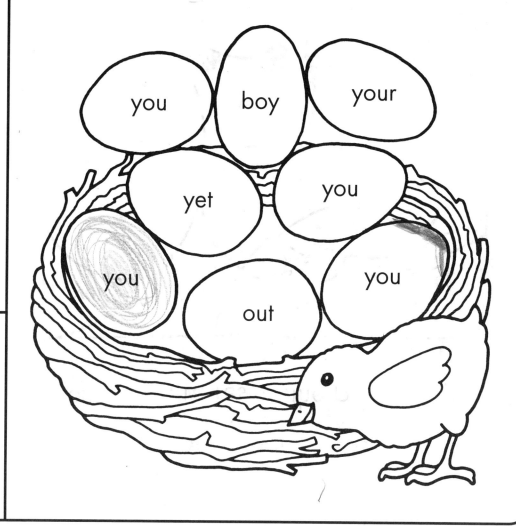

☆208☆ Name: _____

Trace. ✏️

yᴏᴜr

yᴏᴜr

yᴏᴜr

Write **your**.

Find each **your**. Color that puff red.
Then color the rest of the picture.

your

four

your

your

you

our

joy

your